YORK NOTES

General Editors: Professor A.N. Jeffares (*University of Stirling*) & Professor Suheil Bushrui (*American University of Beirut*)

Byron

SELECTED POEMS

Notes by Ian Scott-Kilvert
BA (CAMBRIDGE)

**LONGMAN
YORK PRESS**

YORK PRESS
Immeuble Esseily, Place Riad Solh, Beirut.

ADDISON WESLEY LONGMAN LIMITED
Edinburgh Gate, Harlow,
Essex CM20 2JE, England
Associated companies, branches and representatives
throughout the world

First published 1984
Fifth impression 1996

ISBN 0-582-79250-9

Produced by Longman Singapore Publishers Pte Ltd
Printed in Singapore

Contents

Part 1

Introduction

Life of Byron (1788–1824)

Few writers have lived a life so closely packed with dramatic events as Byron's, and he used his experiences more than most poets do as the raw material for his writings. A bare recital of facts and dates tells little. Some account is needed of Byron's personal qualities, and the interaction of events upon these to explain the complexities of his history.

Byron is the only example in English literature of a poetic genius who was also a peer by inheritance. Hazlitt described him as 'that anomaly in society and letters, a Noble Poet', and this union of seemingly incompatible qualities is reflected in Byron's personality, his history and his art. His moods were notoriously mercurial, now convivial, now withdrawn: he was the cripple who trained himself to be a first-class swimmer and shot, a boxer and an indefatigable traveller: although for most men his creative energy would have filled every waking moment, his temperament craved action rather than writing: he was exceptionally conscious of rank and degree, yet his art was profoundly subversive of established order and privilege. Byron came to be regarded as the very incarnation of the Romantic movement, using 'Romantic' to signify the impulse to assert the personal independence of the individual and the importance of a freer and fuller artistic expression of emotional experience than had been acceptable within the disciplined culture of the preceding century. Yet in his own poetic taste and practice Byron preferred the clarity and decorum of that earlier age, the so-called 'Augustan era': he modelled his writing on the standards of its two great representatives, Dryden and Pope, and was openly contemptuous of much of the verse of his own contemporaries, Wordsworth, Coleridge and Keats.

Byron was born in London on 22 January 1788, the off-spring of a distinguished but often short-lived and doom-laden stock. On the male side the line went back to the de Buruns, Norman followers of William the Conqueror. His father, Captain John Byron, was a dashing Guards officer, whose first wife was the Marchioness of Carmarthen, with whom he eloped in 1779 and who died in 1784: their only surviving child was the poet's half-sister, Augusta. The poet's mother was Catherine Gordon of Gicht, who traced her ancestry to the Stuart kings of

Scotland. The Captain married her in 1785, quickly ran through her capital, fled to France to avoid his creditors, and died in 1791. Meanwhile in 1789 Catherine left London and moved with her baby to Aberdeen, where they were treated as poor relations by their distinguished and wealthy kinsfolk.

Byron's nursemaid was a Scottish girl, May Gray, who taught him to read the Bible and imparted her Calvinist view of religion, but also initiated his sexual education before he was out of the nursery: this early influence bore fruit in Byron's leaning towards the Calvinist doctrine of predestination, according to which God, ever since Adam's fall, has irrevocably divided mankind into the elect, whom he has chosen for salvation, and the damned, who cannot overcome the inborn depravity of human nature. Since May Gray did not apply this stern creed to her personal life, her example strengthened Byron's hatred of hypocrisy. His career is overhung by a continual sense of insecurity and of the capriciousness of destiny. Within three years of his death he could write, 'I have always believed that all things depend upon Fortune and nothing upon ourselves' and this statement helps to explain the opportunism evident in his development as a poet, which marks him out from his fellow Romantics. As the son of a penniless younger son Byron had few expectations, and his early life was spent in a state of poverty which he never forgot. Then, as often in his career, fate intervened. The heir to the fifth Lord was killed in action and Byron inherited the title from his great-uncle. Henceforth, although the family seat at Newstead Abbey, Nottinghamshire, was in ruins, and the estate encumbered with debt, Byron's future was transformed. But this change proved neither easy nor complete. Mrs Byron was a devoted mother, but treated her son, as she had his father, with a mixture of possessive love and uncontrolled exasperation. Despite her noble ancestry, she possessed neither education nor poise, and even by the age of eleven Byron resented her authority and found her an embarrassment.

In 1801 Byron entered Harrow School, where he formed some of his most emotional friendships: he continued to be attracted to adolescent boys for the rest of his life, though this did not hamper his pursuit of the opposite sex even before his teens. After a rough start, when he had to earn respect with his fists, his schooldays were happy. His life-long love of Greece began at Harrow: he read voraciously in history, poetry and fiction, wrote fluent verse, and developed a juvenile talent for acting and oratory.

At seventeen he proceeded to the University of Cambridge. Independence – above all the desire to throw off maternal authority – and pleasure were his objectives rather than learning. His rank entitled him to a degree without examination, and when chided for his frequent absences, he replied, 'Improvement at an English University to a Man of

Rank is, you know, impossible, and the very idea ridiculous.' He read spasmodically, but paid more attention to his obesity, an affliction which beset him all his life: by rigorous dieting and exercise he reduced his weight from over fourteen stone to under ten. In his first year he formed a romantic attachment to John Edleston, a choirboy of Trinity College, whom he records he met every day of his residence, but he was absent from the University so often that he probably spent less than half of his nominal nine terms at Cambridge. He also met two young men who were to become his closest friends, John Cam Hobhouse, later a Whig MP, and Scrope Davies, a classical scholar and a noted wit and gambler during the Regency, the permissive decade (1811–20) when the Prince of Wales assumed the position of Regent, on account of the insanity of George III.

At Cambridge Byron gave more time to his poetry than to his studies. In 1806 he had published at Nottingham *Fugitive Pieces*, containing his earliest poems and some erotic and satirical verses: these provoked a local scandal and he withdrew the book. *Hours of Idleness*, which appeared in 1807, included most of the earlier volume, minus the *risqué* items, for which he substituted some more melancholic and sentimental poems recently composed. Byron's hopes soared when the first notices were favourable, but crashed early in 1808 when the book was savaged by the prestigious *Edinburgh Review*.

Hours of Idleness gives little indication of the achievements to come, but it throws light upon Byron's fatalism and his conviction, even at nineteen, that the best of life was behind him: a surprising number of the poems proclaim the message of lost innocence, lost youth, lost hope. Writing in 1807 to his Harrow friend Edward Long, he confided 'I consider myself as destined never to be happy, though in some instances fortunate. I am an isolated being on earth without a tie to attach me to life, except a few schoolfellows and a score of females.' These moods of melancholy found their outlet in his poems: generally it is his letters which display the exuberant and mocking side of his temperament.

Byron was always resilient, and he quickly launched a counter-attack on *The Edinburgh Review*. *English Bards and Scotch Reviewers* is at once a vindication of the Augustan ideals of wit, reason and propriety, which Byron felt had been unduly devalued by his contemporaries, and a wide-ranging attack on the excesses of the Romantics, in which Wordsworth, Coleridge, Scott, Southey, Mrs Radcliffe and many lesser writers are castigated. The humour is sometimes scurrilous and often schoolboyish, but the poem scores many palpable hits and the author's gusto is infectious. It was well received and Byron could feel that he had levelled the score against the reviewers.

Before he was twenty, Byron's way of living had changed from that of undergraduate to young man of fashion. Unsure of his prospects as a poet, he was determined to assert his independence and increase his knowledge of the world and his standing in it. But he was short of money, and in order to advance, it was necessary to attract notice, hence to live above his means and to borrow. Throughout 1808 he was content to play the prodigal son. 'I am buried in an abyss of sensuality and live in a state of concubinage,' he wrote. He formed a taste for low company, which he kept throughout his life, and enjoyed the society of actresses, boxers and gamblers. Still, even in the abyss, he kept before him two considerable ambitions, to take his seat in the Lords at twenty-one, and to travel abroad.

Both these goals were attained in 1809. Byron's first visit to the Mediterranean was among the most formative experiences of his life and one that distinguishes him from his fellow-Romantics in England. Wordsworth and Coleridge visited France and Germany in modest style for educational and intellectual purposes. Shelley lived in Switzerland and Italy for a combination of personal, medical and legal reasons. Byron's journey was in part an act of liberation from his mother, and from a period of dissipation which had reached its limit. But it was also a version of the aristocratic Grand Tour. True, it was a cut-price expedition since he had to borrow the money from Scrope Davies, and the Napoleonic wars had transformed the tour into a far less ceremonious mode of travel. But at this date Byron could still see himself as a potential orator and statesman, setting out to study men and manners, and the arts of diplomacy and government. He went equipped with servants, presents, letters of introduction and ceremonial uniforms, and obtained passage on any British warship that was going his way.

Together with Hobhouse he first visited Spain, Portugal and Malta, arriving in Greece on a British man-of-war in October 1809. Almost his first journey there was to Ali Pasha, the genial but bloodthirsty ruler of Albania. This encounter made an indelible impression upon Byron. Ali's personality, the barbaric splendour of his court, and the tales of his wars with the wild Souliot tribesmen of north-western Greece provided much of the background for the *Turkish Tales*, and only a few days after leaving Albania he began to write *Childe Harold*. As he travelled south to Athens he was increasingly moved by the contrast between the glories of Greece's past and the degradation of the present under Ottoman rule. The Greek War of Independence was still more than ten years away, and the enforced servility of the people more in evidence than on his second visit. Byron was not blind to the shortcomings of the Greeks, but he admired their frankness, hospitality, and unquenchable desire for freedom. Greece always remained in his memory the land of youthful friendship and adventure. However far away he might be, he wrote in later years, the memory of Greece, passing across his page, 'lifted it into a sudden blaze': there he felt he was living life to the full.

He visited Troy, Istanbul, the Peloponnese, and lingered as long as he could. England offered only disagreeable prospects, a place where he possessed privileges, but lacked the resources to exploit them. Finally he returned in 1811, and at once suffered three crushing blows. His mother died suddenly before he could see her, and because of their estrangement he was overwhelmed with remorse. One of his close Cambridge friends, Charles Matthews, was drowned, and he learned that John Edleston had died during his absence. For some months he drifted in the depths of depression. Meanwhile he was asked what he had written while abroad. He handed over *Hints from Horace*, a conventional literary satire, and then with some reluctance the first two Cantos of *Childe Harold*. His literary go-between, Robert Dallas, read the latter with growing enthusiasm and quickly obtained an acceptance from the rising publishing firm of John Murray. The wheel of fate was about to turn again.

In February 1812 Byron delivered his maiden speech in the House of Lords. He was opposing the Frame-Breaking Bill, which made the smashing of the new mechanical looms (the cause of much unemployment among textile workers) a capital offence. Byron knew the situation at first hand: Nottingham was a textile centre, and the army had already been called in to suppress rioting. He described the fate of the poor in England, a Christian country, as worse than anything he had seen in the most oppressed provinces of infidel Turkey, and he scored a parliamentary triumph. More important, the speech was praised by Lord Holland, the leader of the moderate Whig opposition, and opened to Byron the doors of Holland House, one of the most brilliant intellectual salons in London (Tory society did not compete in cultural matters), and one which Byron had long aspired to enter.

The years of fame

A fortnight after Byron's maiden speech *Childe Harold* was published, and its author 'awoke one morning and found he was famous'. Seven editions sold out in four weeks: it is probably the most instantaneously successful poem ever published in England. A young man's search for experience is an evergreen topic, traditionally the stuff of which bestsellers are made. Although both the poetic autobiography and the travel-poem on the glories of the Mediterranean had been attempted before, none combined the freshness, energy of diction, audacity and easy readability of *Childe Harold*. The moment was ripe for a change, and *Childe Harold* at once created the taste for its special character. Some of the reasons for this are discussed in Part 3 below. In addition, Byron also managed to provoke intense curiosity concerning the personality of the author. He presented a handsome, doom-laden, aristocratic prodigal son in search of adventure, a figure with whom young readers could easily associate themselves, and at the same time he hinted at the identification of the poem's hero with its author, himself handsome, doom-laden, aristocratic, and so on.

The acclaim which greeted *Childe Harold* encouraged Byron to draw upon other recollections from his travels in the *Turkish Tales*. He wrote five of these in the next four years, all best-sellers. They exhibit his gifts as a story-teller in verse, but suffer from having been written at break-neck speed, often in the midst of some crisis in personal relations. Yet despite these spectacular and easy successes, there are grounds for believing that Byron meant much of what he said when he referred to his verse as 'inglorious lays': in other words that until the collapse of his marriage, he continued to think that his prime vocation was to be a politician and public figure, rather than a writer.

At any rate on the social plane Byron had now succeeded beyond his dreams. His lameness and lack of polish were pardoned, and hostesses fought to invite him. His love affair with Lady Caroline Lamb, the young wife of the future Whig Prime Minister Lord Melbourne, begun soon after *Childe Harold* appeared, was an intensely self-conscious performance on both sides. Its significance in Byron's story is that this was the first girl of Byron's own class who had been attracted to him. Lady Caroline was succeeded by the mature Lady Oxford, and for a while Byron enjoyed being courted on all sides, not least by married women, in the permissive society of Regency London.

In the summer of 1813 Byron spent several weeks, more by chance than design, in the company of his half-sister Augusta Leigh to whom he was deeply attached, a married woman with a large family and an absentee husband. What happened remains a mystery, but in August Byron was writing to Tom Moore of 'a strange summer adventure I don't like to think of'. When Augusta's next child was born in April 1814, named Medora after the heroine of the recently published *The Corsair*, Byron could not resist dropping hints about the girl's paternity. Thus a suspicion of a family scandal involving incest was sown in Byron's intimate circle.

In 1814 the reigning and restored monarchs of Europe converged upon London for 'the summer of the sovereigns', a glittering celebration of the downfall of Napoleon and a high-water mark in aristocratic social life which Byron remembered for ever after. Meanwhile his closest friends, including Augusta, had long been urging him to marry, preferably an heiress, since his debts continued to increase. That autumn he proposed to Annabella Milbanke. She was well off, well educated, especially in mathematics, high-principled, and somewhat humourless. She hoped, vainly, to reform him. Byron undoubtedly took pleasure in shocking her.

They were married in January 1815: the union proved disastrous. Byron, still plagued by his creditors, took to drinking heavily and flaunted his association with Augusta. When Annabella's daughter, Ada, was born in January 1816, she took the child to stay with her parents, and although neither husband nor wife had at first intended a break, the situation worsened under family pressure. Annabella never returned, Byron's belated attempts at reconciliation were rejected, and legal arrangements for a separation began. At this point public opinion turned savagely against the poet. When Augusta and Byron attended a party given by the loyal Lady Jersey in the hope of rehabilitating him, Byron's entry gave the cue for most of the guests to leave the room. 'We know of no spectacle so ridiculous as the British public in one of its periodical fits of morality,' wrote Macaulay of these events. In 1812 Byron had been the idol of society: anything could be forgiven to youth, rank and success. Now he found himself remorselessly ostracised, and a fortnight later he left London never to return.

In domestic and social terms the blow was crushing. Byron's hopes of stabilising his personal life and rearing a family were wrecked; he had lost his infant daughter, probably for ever; and the position he valued in the world of aristocracy and fashion had been swept away. His closest friends stood by him, but he was now to be banished from their society and from the companionship that meant most of all to him, Augusta's.

Years of exile

These disasters marked a turning point in Byron's creative life. In London he had sometimes wistfully dreamed of resuming his travels. Now that a wandering life was forced upon him by public disgrace and private distress, the necessity of relieving his feelings spurred him to chronicle his adventures afresh. He took up the mask of *Childe Harold* and in his very first days on the Continent began to compose Canto III.

Byron had ordered for his travels a hugh coach, a Napoleonic model containing a library and dining arrangements: this provided mobility and conspicuous status for the next seven years. He went first to Belgium and visited the battlefield of Waterloo, which inspired the sequence in *Childe Harold*, Canto III (stanzas 17–44), then proceeded up the Rhine valley, reached Geneva in May, and rented a villa by the lake. There he found as his neighbours Shelley – with whom he quickly developed an intellectual companionship such as neither Hobhouse nor his other close friends could offer – Shelley's future wife, Mary Godwin, and her half-sister, Claire Clairmont. Claire had forced her attentions upon Byron during his last weeks in London and early in 1817 bore him a daughter, Allegra. Shelley imparted to Byron some of his enthusiasm for Wordsworth's poetry, which influenced the writing of Canto III. In

June Byron toured the lake with Shelley visiting the towns where Rousseau, Voltaire and Gibbon had lived, which provided material for the later sections of Canto III, and finally the Castle of Chillon. Early in July he finished Canto III and shortly after wrote the blank verse poems *Darkness* and *A Dream*, which reflected the depths of his dejection. Shelley, Mary and Claire returned to England and in September Hobhouse arrived in Geneva and accompanied Byron on a tour of the Bernese Oberland. Byron was deeply moved by the grandeur of the Alps, but confessed that he could not lose his own wretched identity in the majesty of Nature. During this tour he began *Manfred*, the first of his plays, a semi-lyrical drama with a Byronic hero and a Faustian theme.

Byron then set out for Italy. He stayed briefly in Milan, where he met Marie Henri Beyle (1783–1842), later famous as the author of *Le Rouge et le Noir* and *La Chartreuse de Parme*, both written under his pen-name of Stendhal. In November Byron reached Venice, where he was to live for the next three years. He rented an apartment and at once started an affair with his landlord's wife, the pretty Marianna Segati. The Venetian way of life was balm to Byron's state of mind at this time. There was no English colony, both his rank and his literary eminence were duly honoured, and his personal relationships were accepted. Early in 1817 he threw himself into the gaiety of the carnival season, and amid the ensuing excitement and exhaustion composed one of his most perfect lyrics, '*So we'll go no more a-roving*'. Becoming restless in the spring, he travelled through central Italy, met Hobhouse in Rome, and by the late summer had chronicled the emotions and reflections inspired by his journey in Canto IV of *Childe Harold*. While he was still revising and adding to this canto, he read J. H. Frere's mock-heroic *Whistlecraft* and quickly recognised the possibilities of the *ottava rima** stanza for a new type of comic and satirical narrative. The result was *Beppo*, which proved an immediate success in London.

The year 1818 opened with further consolations. Newstead Abbey had been sold and Byron could at last clear his debts. He rented part of the Palazzo Mocenigo on the Grand Canal, and embarked on a season of feverish dissipation, his love affairs forming an amorous catalogue to rival Mozart's Don Juan. Meanwhile he had also begun the first Canto of his last and greatest work, *Don Juan*. Towards the end of it he had written

No more, no more, Oh! never more on me
The freshness of the heart can fall like dew

but very soon afterwards the pattern of his life was again transformed when he fell in love with Teresa Guiccioli, nineteen years old and the

*For a discussion of the *ottava rima*, see Part 3, p. 61.

newly married wife of an elderly Count. This was the famous 'last attachment', broken only by Byron's departure for Greece. Such relationships were an accepted convention of Venetian society. The lover became the *cavaliere servente*, the husband sustaining the legal, the lover the emotional share of the marriage. This was a totally new situation for Byron, but he played his part. He moved to Ravenna, where he lived in a part of the Palazzo Guiccioli rented to him by the Count. Later the husband's patience gave out. A papal separation was obtained, and Teresa went to live with her father, Count Gamba, but Byron's tenancy at the Palazzo remained undisturbed. The Gambas were Liberals and through them Byron became associated with the secret Italian nationalist society, the Carbonari. In 1821 a national uprising against the occupying Austrians seemed imminent, and Byron used his landlord's premises as a secret arsenal for the Carbonari. The rising collapsed, but the Gambas were implicated and forced to seek refuge in Florence, no action being taken against Byron.

These events caused Byron to seek the help of Shelley, who had returned to Italy and now visited Byron at Ravenna: in a letter to his wife he described his friend's eccentric time-table. Byron's day did not begin until about two p.m. He would talk or read with Shelley until six. They would then ride to the forest and practise pistol-shooting, and finally after supper talk until four or five in the morning. It was agreed that Teresa should be invited to move to Pisa, where the Shelleys had settled: a palazzo in the town was rented for Byron, who occupied it in October 1821.

Pisa contained an expatriate intellectual colony. There were Greek political refugees, such as Prince Mavrocordato, who was shortly to take part in the Greek War of Independence: there were several young British ex-officers, the soldiers Edward Williams and Thomas Medwin (who later published his conversations with Byron), and the sailors Daniel Roberts and Edward Trelawny, the latter a living image of Byron's *The Corsair*. Shelley had also invited the radical author Leigh Hunt to join him from London and edit a new literary journal, *The Liberal*. Both poets loved the sea and Roberts and Trelawny helped each to build a boat, but these projects ended tragically in July 1822 when Shelley's boat capsized and he and Williams were drowned. Byron wrote of Shelley to Murray, 'He was the best and least selfish man I ever knew.' After this disaster the colony broke up. The Gambas, again harassed by the authorities, sought refuge in Genoa, where Byron followed them.

Byron's writing in the three years since he had left Venice had been immensely prolific but subject to many changes of plan. The publication of the first two cantos of *Don Juan* in August 1819 provoked a public outcry. Byron was discouraged by his friends' lukewarm support, and so in 1820 turned to other projects. He had written to *Blackwood's*

Magazine attacking the Lake Poets and asserting the superiority of Pope and Dryden to the achievements of modern poetry. He hoped to reinforce the Augustan tradition from another aspect by writing plays on the neo-classical model. *Marino Faliero* was the first of these, the tragedy of a Doge who was executed for siding with the people against the Venetian oligarchy. Byron added Canto V to *Don Juan*, but in 1821 was persuaded by Teresa, who had always disapproved of the poem, to stop work on it. Returning to the drama he wrote *Sardanapalus* and *The Two Foscari*, again with a Venetian background, and *Cain*, a version of the Old Testament story which provided scope for Lucifer to question the divine purpose, the most provocative work Byron had yet attempted. In September 1821 he completed his satirical masterpiece *The Vision of Judgment*, and subsequently three more plays, *Heaven and Hell*, *The Deformed Transformed* and *Werner*: although these were composed on strict neo-classical principles, they are the weakest of Byron's dramas.

Shortly before Shelley's death Byron resumed work on *Don Juan*, and Leigh Hunt describes how Byron would laughingly read aloud to Teresa in Italian the parts he wished her to hear. He had become convinced of the poem's satirical potential, and now carried out the most sustained creative effort of his life. By the end of 1822 he had completed Cantos VI–XII, and in the spring of 1823 Cantos XIII–XVI and the unfinished Canto XVII, by which time he had decided to join the Greek cause. Meanwhile Murray became more and more lukewarm about the poem, and finally Byron sent the manuscripts to be published by Leigh Hunt's brother John.

Byron's last residence in Italy was in Genoa, where he joined Teresa in October 1822. The city was something of a backwater, and he began to consider another change – to return to Greece or emigrate to South America. The scene was unexpectedly enlivened in April 1823 by the visit of the Earl and Countess of Blessington, the latter celebrated alike for her beauty and her intelligence. Byron had met no such brilliant representative of London society throughout his exile, and her company recalled what he had lost. She later published the most lively of all the records of Byron's conversations. Meanwhile the London Greek Committee, of which Hobhouse was a member, had approached Byron to support the national uprising. Byron offered to visit the provisional Greek Government to assess the needs of the cause. But he knew the pain that this would cause Teresa, and at first shrank from declaring his plans. In May he decided, and invited Trelawny, Teresa's young brother Pietro and an Italian physician, Dr Bruno, to accompany him. They sailed from Genoa in July.

The Greek rebellion was never a unified effort, but was riven by local and political divisions, so that no leader could enter rival territory.

There were the guerilla chiefs in the mountains, who possessed military experience and operated as independent warlords. There were westernised intellectuals, such as Mavrocordato, who could attract international goodwill, but lacked military capacity, and, as in the Spanish civil war in the 1930s, the great powers manoeuvred behind the scenes. Byron discerned these rivalries with more acumen than the philhellenic idealists of the London Committee, especially when he found himself courted by all the leaders in turn. He halted at the Ionian island of Cephalonia to gather information before committing himself to any one faction. There he met Colonel Napier, the British Resident, who convinced him that with a few hundred trained men he could transform the fortunes of the Greeks. Byron recommended Colonel Napier to the Committee, and while he himself contributed to the limits of his income, he urged the raising of a commercial loan. The first proposal was rejected, the second bore immediate fruit. Finally Byron decided to join Mavrocordato and arrived at Missolonghi in January 1824: the whole population thronged to the quay-side and greeted him as a Messiah.

Missolonghi was a small fishing port in western Greece, plagued by a malarious climate. It was the headquarters of Mavrocordato and the rallying point for the Philhellenes, many of them European officers, prematurely retired after Waterloo, who had come to Greece to find employment. Once he had thrown in his lot with Mavrocordato, only time would show whether Byron's role would be that of administrator of the loan, leader of irregulars, or 'shuttle-diplomat' between the Greek factions. Meanwhile there were three immediate prospects – the raising of a trained force under Napier, the arrival of a team of artillery technicians from London, equipped with Congreve rockets, and an early attack on the nearby Turkish fortress of Lepanto: for this last project Byron enrolled and maintained five hundred Souliots, refugee members of the warrior tribe of Epirus. All three schemes collapsed. Napier was turned down in London: the technicians achieved little and demanded to be sent home: the Souliots mutinied for higher pay, so that the Lepanto operation never materialised.

In February Byron suffered an attack of epilepsy, but recovered and struggled on against all the odds, directing the European officers in their training, striving to reconcile the quarrelling Greeks and foreigners, soldiers and civilians. It is ironical that while in his London years Byron had been repelled by the party manoeuvrings and patient committee work which would have been required if he were to build himself a political career, in Greece, although often angry at the intrigue and muddle of his surroundings, he handled with firmness and realism the petty details that were thrust upon him: he had become a father figure to the cause. He insisted on riding out with the troops to keep up the morale of the townspeople, and on 9 April was caught in a heavy downpour. He developed a fever which mounted rapidly, and his inexperienced doctors treated him only by bleeding and purging which rapidly undermined his strength. It was proposed to move him to the island of Zante, or bring over an English doctor, but a violent storm cut off all communication. He died on 19 April. His death, amid these scenes of military frustration and medical incompetence is sometimes represented as a tragic waste. Yet it was his determination to remain in an apparently hopeless situation which made the sacrifice priceless, and won over public opinion throughout Europe to the Greek cause.

A note on the text

The complete poems and extracts discussed in these notes, with the exception of the lyric 'The Isles of Greece', are included in *Selected Poems of Byron*, edited by Robin Skelton, Poetry Bookshelf Series, Heinemann Educational Books, London, 1964 (reprinted 1980) and the texts quoted are all taken from this edition. Until recently the standard edition of Byron's poetical works was that of E. H. Coleridge in six volumes, Murray, London, 1898–1904, based on *The Works of Lord Byron* (1831). This is now being superseded by *The Complete Poetical Works* edited by Professor J. J. McGann, published by the Clarendon Press, Oxford. Seven volumes have appeared to date, including the whole of *Childe Harold* and *Don Juan* The standard edition of the *Letters and Journals* is that of Professor L.A. Marchand in twelve volumes, Murray, London, 1973–82.

Part 2

Summaries
of SELECTED POEMS

'I would I were a careless child'

The poet looks back with regret to the carefree years of his childhood. He longs to renounce the privileges which birth and inheritance have conferred on him. These have brought only an illusory well-being, ending in solitude, and he pines for the less ambitious but more genuine friendships he once knew.

COMMENTARY: The poem was probably written in late 1807. The theme of a lost paradise which a child must leave behind as he grows up is a commonplace of Romantic poetry. From 1789 to 1798, when he inherited his title, Byron lived in poverty with his mother in Aberdeen. In 1796 he spent a summer holiday in the valley of the Dee and came to love the Highland scenery of Loch-na-Gar and the mountains surrounding Deeside: he thus associates these memories with a time of innocence and simple pleasures. When Byron prepared the second edition of *Hours of Idleness* he added this and other sentimental pieces: this self-pitying note in the volume was a factor which attracted the blistering attack in the *Edinburgh Review*.

NOTES AND GLOSSARY:

my Highland cave: through his mother Byron was descended from the Highland clan of the Gordons

The cumbrous pomp of Saxon pride: the phrase expresses the Highlander's traditional animosity to the heavy-handed domination which the English monarchy had imposed at various periods of Scottish history

Fortune! take back: when Byron became the sixth Baron his inheritance included estates in Nottinghamshire and Lancashire

Fain would I fly: this line, the next three and those of the fourth stanza foreshadow the image which Byron was to project in the personality of Childe Harold, that of the gloomy outcast who takes refuge in travel, because he has exhausted the pleasures of the senses and has built no worth-while human relationship

Oh! that to me: these final four lines are adapted from Psalm 55:6. Byron noted that 'this verse also constitutes part of the most beautiful anthem in our language'. He wrote this poem as an undergraduate, and it is likely that the lines allude to the singing of the Trinity chorister John Edleston, to whom he was devoted

'Written after swimming from Sestos to Abydos'

In this playfully ironic lyric Byron compares his experience and his motives in swimming the Hellespont to those of the earlier legendary swimmer, Leander: both are punished by the gods, Leander by drowning, Byron by an attack of fever.

COMMENTARY: In May 1810, after wintering in Athens, Byron travelled to Smyrna. There he obtained passage on HMS Salsette, a frigate bound for Istanbul. He visited the plain of Troy and resolved to fulfil a long-cherished ambition to swim the Hellespont. After one unsuccessful attempt he made the crossing with Lieutenant William Ekenhead of the Royal Marines. Byron was extremely proud of this feat.

NOTES AND GLOSSARY:

Leander, Hero: according to the legend first immortalised by the Greek poet Musaeus (fifth–sixth century AD) and later by the Roman poet Ovid (43BC-AD17) and the English dramatist Christopher Marlowe (1564–93), Hero, a virgin priestess of Aphrodite at Sestos on the European shore of the channel, fell in love with Leander, who lived at Abydos. He wooed her by nightly swimming the straits guided by a light in her tower. One stormy night the light was blown out: Leander was drowned and Hero drowned herself

'To Thomas Moore'

This genial drinking song is dedicated to Byron's close friend, Thomas Moore (1779–1852), the Irish poet who was to become his biographer. The poem was started in April 1816, just before Byron left England – hence the imagery of a voyage about to begin – and completed in July 1817. Byron noted that he composed it after swimming in the Adriatic 'with a black-eyed Venetian girl before me, reading Boccaccio'. The poet avows his resolve to drink his friend's health, whatever changes fortune may bring.

'Stanzas to Augusta'

The poet declares his gratitude to his sister for her comfort, support and understanding at the time of the break-up of his marriage and his ostracism by London society. When Fortune and his wife abandoned him, Augusta alone remained constant, although the cloud of slander threatened her own reputation. Whatever disasters may befall him, she and her child will be unharmed and rewarded by Heaven. While she and her love are there, the earth will not be a desert, even for Byron.

COMMENTARY: This poem, composed in April 1816, was probably the last that Byron wrote before leaving England. It is one of a group of 'poems of separation', occasioned by the events which culminated in his legal separation from his wife. Some of the earlier poems dwell on the intensity of the feeling which united Byron and Augusta: here the dominant note is one of tenderness and gratitude for her loyalty.

NOTES AND GLOSSARY:

the cloud: a reference to the rumours that they were guilty of incest

to brave or brook: to defy or tolerate

'So, we'll go no more a-roving'

This poem, written in February 1817 at the end of Byron's first carnival season in Venice, was enclosed in a letter to Tom Moore. Byron remarked that he had found the sword wearing out the sheath, though he had but just turned the corner of twenty-nine.

COMMENTARY: The refrain is associated with an Aberdeenshire ballad: 'And I'll gang nae mair a-rovin'. Byron's lyrics are often inspired by a particular person or event, but this one carries something of the universality of the ballad genre. Though apparently straightforward in sense, it is also one of the subtlest of Byron's lyrics. It can be regarded either as a soliloquy, or as an exchange between lovers. In the first case 'we' denotes the first person singular, a recognition that the poet has reached a moment in life when he no longer wishes to sustain the pursuit or exploration of love. 'A-roving' in this sense (twice rhymed with 'loving') suggests the incessant search for a new partner: it echoes the description Byron gives of himself in *Childe Harold*, 'this wayward, loveless heart', and anticipates *Don Juan*, Canto I, in the following year

No more, no more, Oh! never more on me
The freshness of the heart can fall like dew

The dialogue theory offers a richer interpretation. 'So', followed by a comma, introduces a note of irony – 'Very well, this is the situation, then'. 'A-roving', in the Venetian context, can suggest romantic visits by gondola in carnival time, to balls, parties, apartments, or perhaps *à deux* – 'into the night'. 'So late' evokes the phase in the relationship when time was forgotten, echoed in 'and the day returns too soon'.

There is an antithesis between the two adjectives in this stanza, 'loving' referring to the warmth and vulnerability of the heart, 'bright' to the glamorous but cold light of the moon. In the second stanza, the mood shifts to one of satiety, perhaps momentary, perhaps permanent: the rhymes 'sheathe', 'breathe', 'breast', 'rest', exhale a sigh of exhaustion. The affair requires a pause – to separate or to consolidate? The third stanza may be read as a summing-up. Though the elements which created the love are still there, the heart and the night, yet a change has taken place, perhaps just the passage of time, the end of the first passionate impetus. The future will not be the same.

Throughout the poem, Byron uses the impersonal definite article – 'the heart', 'the soul', and so on – not the possessive pronoun, a choice which again hints at the universality of the ballad style.

The Corsair (1813)

The Corsair is among Byron's longer verse tales, but the passage selected contains only some fifty lines from the last Canto: to explain this episode requires a summary of the plot as a whole.

Canto 1: The pirates' creed is explained – the choice of a life of lawless freedom, danger and high rewards. The scene is the Aegean island lair, where Conrad, their leader, has decided to sail against the Turks that night. His disposition is not evil by nature, but has been embittered by early misfortune: 'Lone, wild and strange he stood, alike exempt/From all affection and from all contempt'. This harsh exterior is softened only by his love for his mistress, Medora. When he takes his leave of the lonely girl, she begs him to abandon piracy and share the joys of peace. But he sees her craving for security as a threat to his self-sufficiency and powers of leadership, and explains the paradox in his nature, 'I cease to love thee when I love mankind'. Vowing his devotion, he nevertheless departs.

Canto II: A banquet is being held by Seyd, the Turkish pasha whom Conrad is about to attack. Conrad enters, disguised as an escaped prisoner of the corsairs, and while Seyd questions him, the assault begins. The first onslaught succeeds, but when Conrad tries to rescue the women of the pasha's harem, the impetus is lost and the attackers are wiped out. Conrad is condemned to death by impalement. Gulnare, the favourite in Seyd's harem, falls in love with the prisoner because of his passion for freedom – 'I felt, I feel, love dwells with – with the free'. Conrad is touched by her devotion, but fears lest 'the unanswerable tear in woman's eye' will unman him.

Canto III: The few survivors of the raid return to their island. Medora faints on hearing the news. In Seyd's palace Gulnare begs the pasha to ransom Conrad. He suspects her motives and refuses. Gulnare visits

Conrad's cell, offering him a dagger to kill Seyd. Conrad rejects this plan as treacherous, whereupon Gulnare stabs the pasha herself. This abandonment of her feminine role, and the consequent humiliation of owing his life to a woman, transforms Gulnare for ever in Conrad's eyes. He returns to the island (Part xxi) to find that Medora, believing him killed, has died of grief. Her death annihilates Conrad's softer feelings: his whole capacity to respond to another being had been concentrated in this relationship. As the metaphor in lines 50–7 of the passage indicates, his heart of granite, capable of sheltering one blossom, is now shattered into fragments. The story of Conrad's and Gulnare's later adventures is told in *Lara*.

COMMENTARY: *The Giaour*, *The Bride of Abydos* and *The Corsair* were the first three of the five *Turkish Tales*, verse novelettes with which Byron followed up the success of *Childe Harold*. All three were completed in 1813, *The Bride* reputedly in four days, *The Corsair* in ten. The latter was received even more enthusiastically than *Childe Harold*, ten thousand copies being sold on the first day. All five are adventure stories set in the Mediterranean or Near East: in *The Giaour* and *The Corsair* the age-old clash between Christian and Moslem is intensified by rivalry in love. The psychology of the heroes of these tales is discussed in Part 3. In creating such figures, Byron was at once indulging a personal fantasy and weaving a personal legend. He certainly knew of, may even have met, the type of European sailor of fortune – smuggler or privateer – who flourished by blockade-running during the Napoleonic wars (compare the hero of Ernest Hemingway's (1899–1961) novel *To Have and To Have Not*): his journal records that *The Corsair* 'was written *con amore* and much from existence'. He liked to imagine himself as a man of action, and he dropped hints in his correspondence and conversation of experiences of illicit passion and adventure gathered during his travels. 1813 was a year of emotional disturbance for Byron. He wrote of *The Bride of Abydos*, which skirts the margin of the theme of incest, 'My mind has been from late . . . events in such a state of fermentation that I have been obliged to empty it in rhyme. This is my usual resource.' *The Corsair* was written six weeks later.

NOTES AND GLOSSARY:

he deserved his fate: these words recall Medora's plea to Conrad in Canto I to abandon piracy and commit himself to a shared future

in that one: in that one joy

the refuge found in none: the sufferer cannot find refuge in even one consoling thought

like that had harden'd too: the metaphor is of drops of water in a cave hardening into stalactites

If such his heart:	if his heart were of rock
blacken:	the meaning here is: 'only shivered fragments of the once protective rock now blacken on the barren ground'

Hebrew Melodies (1815)

In June 1814 Isaac Nathan, a Jewish music publisher, invited Byron to contribute lyrics to a collection of Hebrew melodies he had discovered, which he claimed had been sung by the Jews before the destruction of the temple of Jerusalem (AD70). Byron composed a number of poems that autumn and continued the series in early 1815, immediately after his marriage. The poems he finally gave to Nathan included several – of which 'She walks in beauty' is the best known – which had been written before the scheme was proposed, and have no apparent connection with it.

When Nathan published his collection in 1815 under the title *A Selection of Hebrew Melodies*, he was following a fashion which had started some twenty years before. There had been *A Collection of Scottish Airs* with lyrics by Burns, followed by various anthologies of Irish melodies, some with lyrics by Moore. Moore was especially active in composing poems concerning lost freedom and nationalist aspirations and Byron readily championed the cause of subject peoples.

Compared with his contemporaries Byron is not regarded as a master of the lyric. With rare exceptions his verse excels at the clear, firmly struck note of the brass, but lacks the lingering delicacy of the wood-wind. *Hebrew Melodies* is the fruit of the one period when he applied himself continuously to lyrical composition and provides the best example of his lyrical range. It is a heterogeneous collection which contains love-songs, elegies, reflections on mortality and martial lays. Poems such as 'O snatched away' and 'My soul is dark' (on the power of music) were inspired by thoughts of Edleston, and it has been argued that the volume was a hidden tribute to the dead chorister: but themes based on the Old Testament and later Jewish history naturally predominate. These poems are by no means devotional or pious in tone, but they testify to the Calvinistic strain implanted in Byron during his Aberdeen boyhood. The theme of exile, always a central topic for him, pervades 'On Jordan's Banks', 'On the Day of the Destruction of Jerusalem' and 'By the Rivers of Babylon'. Supernatural prophecy and occult knowledge (later explored in *Manfred*) are the subject of 'Saul' and 'A Spirit passed before me', while 'The Destruction of Sennacherib', 'The Song of Saul before his last Battle' and 'The Vision of Belshazzar' deal with the complex and awesome relation of Jehovah to his Chosen People.

'She walks in beauty' *Hebrew Melodies*

At a ball in June 1814 Byron met Mrs Wilmot Horton, the wife of his second cousin. She was in mourning and did not dance: since he himself could not dance because of his malformed foot, this may have given Byron a feeling of affinity. The spangles worn on Mrs Wilmot's black dress made a strong impression on Byron, who wrote the poem the next day. The vision which the subject inspires combines the beauties of night and of day. The darkness of her dress and of her hair symbolises the one, the light which radiates from her face, eyes and expression the other, and the two elements are perfectly balanced. The beauty of her physical appearance is matched by the spiritual qualities of which it is an expression. In one of his conversations with Lady Blessington, Byron remarked, 'I do not talk of mere beauty of feature or complexion, but of expression, that looking out of the soul through the eyes which in my opinion constitutes true beauty.'

'The Destruction of Sennacherib' *Hebrew Melodies*

Written shortly after Byron's marriage: the source is the Bible, II Kings 18–19. The Jewish king Hezekiah refused the demand for surrender made by Sennacherib's emissary, and prayed for deliverance from the Assyrian invasion: Jehovah's answer to his prayer was conveyed by the prophet Isaiah: 'He shall not come into this city, saith the Lord.' The Bible goes on to describe the destruction of the Assyrian army: 'And it came to pass that the Angel of the Lord went out and smote in the camp of the Assyrians an hundred fourscore and five thousand, and in the morning behold they were all dead corpses.'

COMMENTARY: The poem is a good example of Byron's ability to cast a lyric in a powerful narrative form. The metaphors chosen – the leaves, first green, then withered, the fever-wracked foam of the horses, the dew on the rider's brow, motionless lance, melted snow, are all simple, concrete, intensely vivid: the anapaestic foot (two short, one long syllable) gives the poem a ballad-like impetus, and concentrates the stress on the monosyllabic nouns which dominate the imagery – surf, rust, tents, snow.

NOTES AND GLOSSARY:

cohorts: a Roman military term for a unit about three hundred men strong

sheen: flashing

'A Spirit passed before me' *Hebrew Melodies*

The poem is a versified paraphrase of Job 4:15–20. The words are spoken by Eliphaz the Temanite, one of Job's three friends whose advice fails to comfort him. In Chapter 1 of the Book of Job Satan obtains leave from God to test Job's faith, since, as he claims, 'But ... touch all that he hath, and he will curse thee to they face.' Eliphaz's message is that Job's afflictions are really for his own good – 'happy is the man whom God correcteth.' He describes the vision he has seen in the night, and quotes the words of the Spirit, which were, 'Shall mortal man be more just than God? shall a man be more pure than his maker? Behold, he put no trust in his servants, and his angels he charged with folly: How much less in them that dwell in houses of clay, whose foundation is in the dust, which are crushed before the moth?' In other words, Job's presumption in questioning his afflictions is rebuked, since man is a sinful, short-lived creature, weaker even than the moth, that feeds on decay.

This problem – how is it right for God, having created man weak, to punish him for his weakness? – never ceased to torment Byron, and he takes the question a stage further in *Cain*. Lucifer assures Cain that 'He is great/But in his greatness is no happier than/We in our conflict: goodness would not make/Evil; And what else hath he made?'

The Prisoner of Chillon (1816)

The poem was inspired by Byron's visit with Shelley to the castle of Chillon at the end of June 1816, and was finished ten days later. Byron's sonnet on Chillon, 'Eternal spirit of the chainless mind', was composed later in the year after he had read more of the prisoner's history. François Bonivard (1496–1570), scholar, historian and satirist, was the prior of the monastery of St Victor near Geneva. He belonged to the party which strove to free the city from the rule of the Duke of Savoy and establish its political and religious independence. He was imprisoned without trial for six years (1530–36), four of which he spent in the dungeon.

Sections I–VIII: The prisoner describes how his family was persecuted for continuing his father's struggle to defend the liberties of Geneva. Of his five brothers one was executed, two killed in battle, two imprisoned with him. The three captives were chained to pillars in a dungeon only dimly penetrated by daylight. The second brother was a huntsman, the third his father's favourite. François, as the eldest, strives to comfort the others, but the tomb-like darkness of their prison below the waters of the lake oppresses the spirits of all three. The huntsman, least prepared for captivity, dies first. Next the youngest brother yields to despair and breathes his last. François is left alone, sustained only by the faith which forbids him to succumb. His state of mind – 'I know not why/I could not die' – echoes that of Coleridge's Ancient Mariner, as he watched his shipmates perish one by one.

Sections IX–XIV: The prisoner passes into a trance-like state in which he can register neither light nor darkness, sound nor the passage of time. He is restored to consciousness by the song of a bird, which alights on the dungeon window: the sound brings back his sight and his capacity for feeling. He fancies the bird may embody the soul of his brother, but then it takes flight, returning him to his solitary thoughts. His gaolers now show more compassion, and allow him to move about the dungeon. He makes a foothold in the wall and peers out of the embrasure. He glimpses the snow-clad mountains, the blue Rhône, the white-walled town opposite, a tiny island, and birds and fish as they move at liberty. His melancholy returns and the gloom of the prison closes over him as if it were a newly dug grave. Again he loses all sense of time until finally his liberators arrive. But by then he is scarcely aware of the difference between confinement and freedom: he has converted his prison into a refuge from the world. Contemplating his humble fellow creatures, spiders and mice, he has felt no desire to exercise his superior power. He has accepted his chains as a part of himself, so that finally 'I/Regain'd my freedom with a sigh'.

COMMENTARY: *The Prisoner* is unlike any other of Byron's *Tales*, and modern commentators have been sharply divided in judging its merits. It has been described as the best of all his non-satirical verse narratives, as an unskilful imitation of a tale of the Lake school type, as a superior 'tear-jerker'. What clearly distinguishes *The Prisoner* from the earlier tales is its detachment, its creation of a hero who is in no way identified with the poet, its insight into sufferings of which Byron had no experience, its pursuit of a new kind of realism which does not merely seek to entertain the reader. The subject of long imprisonment imposed by a tyrannical authority, and tantamount to living burial, was popular in Romantic art, Ludwig von Beethoven's (1770–1827) *Fidelio* being a notable example. Byron's treatment is different, and anticipates what he was to do later in the shipwreck sequence (Canto II) of *Don Juan*, namely to represent, without illusion or happy ending, what such an ordeal would really be like. The *Turkish Tales* had offered spectacular scenery, stirring action, mystery, surprising twists of the plot. The story of *The Prisoner* is unrelievedly cheerless; it is saved from monotony by the unrelenting honesty with which Byron explores his theme. He does not, as might be imagined from the Chillon sonnet, pay homage to the power of the human spirit to hold out against the mental and physical torture of long confinement: on the contrary the poem is a record of the permanent damage such sufferings can inflict.

The shortest of the tales, *The Prisoner* gains from its compactness: unlike some of the weaker tales it repays close reading. The irreparable damage done to Bonivard is announced at once: mentally the marks of the iron will not wear away 'Till I have done with this new day', that is, until death. Sections VII and VIII describe how life is gradually crushed out of his brothers. The prisoner's own isolation culminates in Section IX with the loss of almost all his faculties. When he recovers perception of the sights and sounds of Nature, it is too late. His consciousness can only register the shape of his dungeon – 'The whole earth would henceforth be/A wider prison unto me'.

At this time Byron was susceptible to the influence of Wordsworth's verse, and the diction and metre of *The Prisoner* illustrate this more clearly than *Childe Harold*, Canto III. The habit of repetitive statement employed elsewhere in the tales, here takes on the Lake school style. The islet is described (lines 346–9) with a similar enumeration of simple, even trite epithets and images:

> But in it there were three tall trees,
> And o'er it blew the mountain breeze,
> And by it there were waters flowing,
> And on it there were young flowers growing.

This mode of description recurs throughout the poem. Compared with the effects which Coleridge achieves with a similarly simple vocabulary, Byron's choice of noun and epithet often sounds flat. Only rarely, as in 'Had seen the mice at moonlight play', does he create an arresting image. The poem deals with a static situation, and its power, unique in Byron's writing, lies in the truth of the skilfully prepared anticlimax. The prisoner, when suddenly and arbitrarily released, has lost the will to live at liberty.

Childe Harold's Pilgrimage: Canto IV   (1817)

In 1817 Byron visited Rome and other famous Italian cities, including Florence and Ferrara. Returning to Venice in May, he wrote the first draft of Canto IV in July (126 stanzas): a further sixty were added in the autumn, making this the longest Canto of the four. Of the three passages selected here the first two were among these later additions. The third is an expanded version of the invocation to Ocean, which concludes the poem. Because of these additions the interweaving of public and private themes is exceptionally intricate: this aspect of Canto IV is dealt with in commentaries immediately following the summaries of the three passages: the poem is discussed as a whole in Part 3.

Stanzas 93–8: What is the harvest of man's limited potentialities in a world where life is short, truth elusive and the force of opinion strong but fallible, so that men lose faith in their own free judgments? For this reason the human race always remains in a state of slavery, yet is always willing to defend the *status quo*. Byron is not here discussing religious faith but the political process. Is revolution merely an exchange of tyrants? The French Revolution, which began in 1789, proved fatal to men's liberties, yet the cause of freedom is not dead: its seeds are still being sown.

COMMENTARY: These added stanzas expand the theme which begins in stanzas 82–92, a review of Roman history. The argument starts from the eternal conflict between the claims of liberty, just government and political ambition: it considers the examples of Cromwell and Napoleon, 'a bastard Caesar' (stanzas 90–2) and then surveys contemporary history. Byron laments the apparently unbreakable sequence of oppression and voluntary servitude which mankind accepts, but reaffirms his faith in the unconquerable spirit of freedom.

NOTES AND GLOSSARY:

being: existence

Our senses narrow: this line and the rest of the stanza paraphrase the Roman orator and politician Cicero's (106–43BC) *Academica*, Ch. 13. The ancient Greek philosophers, that is, those before Socrates, had argued that knowledge could not be obtained through the senses

Opinion an omnipotence: the irresistible force of public opinion. Possibly an allusion to the social ostracism which had forced Byron to leave England

The yoke ... doubly bow'd: an allusion to the Holy Alliance formed in 1816 between Russia, Austria and Prussia. By this pact the powers of the rulers of the three great monarchies were reaffirmed by reference to their divine as well as their hereditary right to rule

Columbia: the name is used to personify the United States as the new birthplace of liberty created by the American War of Independence

Pallas: the goddess both of wisdom and of war, who in Greek mythology was born fully grown and armed from the head of Zeus

Saturnalia: a Roman festival held in December to commemorate the Golden Age of Saturn, before he was supplanted as ruler of the gods by Jupiter. During these days slaves could speak freely and ridicule their masters: the word here signifies a time of unlimited anarchy and licence

the base pageant: a reference to the pomp of the Congress of Vienna held in 1816, which reversed many of the changes effected in Europe by Napoleon and turned the clock back in favour of the restored monarchies

his second fall: this may refer to man's political ruin, which follows his first loss (expulsion from Eden)

against **the wind:** contrary to the apparent momentum of events

The loudest still the tempest leaves behind: those who stand behind the trumpeter can hear his notes magnified by the storm which blows them back

the bosom of the North: the allusion is obscure: it could be to the example of America, or in the Italian context it might refer back to stanza 47, which foretold that Italy, now oppressed by Austria, would be freed by Europe

Stanzas 122–35: The train of thought begins earlier, at stanza 115, with the Roman myth of Egeria, the nymph who imparted her divine love to the mortal king Numa. Human love is not of such quality. This fact reminds Byron of the illusions of beauty or of ideal relationships conceived in youth and vainly pursued in manhood. Life is really a perpetual withering, but we continue to be lured by imaginary objects of desire – love, fame, ambition, wealth. Yet though we are predestined to sin and disappointment, we must always cling to the faculty of independent thought, and in time the light of truth will return. Contemplating the remains of the Coliseum, Byron identifies his own fortunes with the ruined arena and reflects on the power of Time and Nature to heal wounds and beautify ruins. He recalls his sufferings, but refuses to seek revenge: that he leaves to Nemesis. He offers forgiveness, which in itself will prove a curse to his enemies.

COMMENTARY: Stanza 135 was a late addition, which by introducing the theme of forgiveness, modifies the preceding six. The thoughts inspired by the Coliseum repeatedly mingle with personal memories and emotions and the sequence needs to be read in context with stanzas 136–51. Stanzas 128–30 echo the thought first voiced on the Acropolis (Canto II, stanzas 2, 6, 10) that Time magically transforms Art, turning ruins into works of nature. In stanza 131 Byron identifies his own destiny with the ruins (compare Canto IV, stanza 25). His prayer to Time and Nemesis to avenge his wrongs begins with stanza 130 and culminates in stanzas 135–7: the last stanza foretells that Byron's endurance will in the end soften hearts which are as hard as rock now. Nemesis is also associated with the gladiator sequence (stanzas 139–42), which illustrates the cruelty of Rome and the retribution that followed: the gladiators were drawn from the subject peoples, who finally overwhelmed the empire. The imagery is also linked to Byron's wrongs:

his private life was butchered by society to make a Roman holiday. The theme of forgiveness, stated in stanza 135, culminates with the story of the Roman girl (stanzas 148–51), who saves the life of her imprisoned father by feeding him from her breast.

NOTES AND GLOSSARY:

with a crutch-like rod: the god Circumstance is shown in the same guise as Nemesis, who, although lame, never fails to overtake the wrong-doer

upas . . . tree: a tree found in Java, believed to be so poisonous that it could destroy all life within a radius of fifteen miles

Yet let us ponder: this appeal to the value of the reasoning faculty paraphrases a passage in Sir William Drummond's (1585–1649) *Academical Questions*, I, 14

couch: a term in ophthalmic surgery: to remove a cataract by downward displacement of the lens of the eye

Arches on arches: the first, second and third tiers of the Coliseum comprised eighty arches to each storey, in the Doric, Ionic and Corinthian styles respectively

Oh Time! the beautifier: when Byron saw Rome, the ruins of the Coliseum were covered with luxuriant shrubs and wild flowers

Nemesis: a Greek divinity also worshipped by the Romans and associated with fortune and retribution. The reference to homage is to Augustus (63BC–AD14), the Roman Emperor, who is said to have disguised himself once a year as a beggar and sat at his palace gate

the Furies . . . Orestes: these lines may contain an allusion to Byron's wife. He named her 'My moral Clytaemnestra', referring to the Greek queen of Argos, who killed her husband Agamemnon for his infidelity. Their son Orestes avenged his father by killing her, whereupon the spirit of Clytaemnestra called upon the Furies to haunt Orestes and drive him mad

Stanzas 177–86: At the end of his pilgrimage, the poet looks down from high ground towards the sea. He longs to withdraw from society and live with one companion alone. He addresses the Ocean as the element most congenial to his spirit. It is the primal element, which resists man's incursions and destructive impulses. Its power is limitless: it has remained unchanged since the dawn of creation. Yet it has borne the poet from his childhood upward, gently and safely upon its billows.

NOTES AND GLOSSARY:

one fair spirit: the allusion is probably to Byron's half-sister Augusta

oak leviathans: battleships of the largest size

spoils of Trafalgar: this refers to the gale which sprang up soon after the battle and destroyed many of the captured French and Spanish ships

sandal shoon and scallop shells: the sandals on his feet and the scallop shells in his hat were the traditional badges of the mediaeval pilgrim to the shrine of St James of Compostella in Spain. The words refer back to the beginning of Canto I, where Childe Harold is described as setting out in the garb of a pilgrim

---

'The Isles of Greece' (1821)

Byron invokes the beauty of the isles, radiant in the Aegean sunlight, but reflects that the glorious achievements of the Greeks are all in the past. Musing over the scenes of the battles of Marathon and Salamis, he asks how Greece can endure her present enslavement. The voices of the dead reply, and ask for a single worthy living descendant to come forth. 'Fill high the cup' is the poet's comment: how much easier to drown sorrows in revelry than to rebel. Yet even now the examples of Suli and Parga prove that the Greek spirit lives on. But do not trust foreign liberators: Greece must regain her freedom with her own hands. The poet retires for consolation to Cape Sunium, with its panoramic view of the isles. Throughout the song he is tormented by the paradox that the splendour of the landscape, the beauty of the girls as they dance, the revelry of Haidée's intended wedding-feast will bring forth only a race of slaves.

COMMENTARY: This poem, a continuation of stanza 86 of Canto III of *Don Juan*, embodies Byron's most ardent affirmation of the glories of Greece, her natural beauty, her achievements in war and civilisation, and her love of freedom. It is an even more striking example of the 'national melodies' type of lyric, which we find in *Hebrew Melodies*, an appeal to the native heroism of an oppressed people. As in *Childe Harold* Byron introduces a lyrical interlude, partly to dramatise a character or situation, partly to change the mood of the narrative, so here he introduces a powerful and unexpected contrast in the narrative. The occasion for the song is the romantic banquet given by Haidée to celebrate her unofficial union with Juan. But the song itself is introduced as the work of the local ballad-monger, a thinly disguised caricature of Byron's pet aversion, Southey: 'his muse made increment of anything'. It has been persuasively argued that the lyric had been written some nine years before Canto III, namely during Byron's first visit to Greece. His habit of immediate composition on the scene of his travels lends weight to this theory (he never again saw Marathon or Salamis). Also his ironical view of the Greeks' prospects of regaining their freedom is much more understandable at the earlier date than on the eve of the War of Independence.

NOTES AND GLOSSARY:

Sappho: a poetess famous for her erotic verse, who lived on the island of Lesbos in the late sixth century BC. Although her work survives only in fragments, she is among the greatest of the Greek lyrical poets

Delos a tiny island in the centre of the Cyclades. According to legend it was the birthplace of Apollo, god of the sun and patron deity of the Delphic oracle and of literature, art, music and science

Scian . . . muse: Scios is another name for Chios, one of the reputed birthplaces of Homer

Teian: Teos was the birthplace of Anacreon, a much admired lyric poet of the sixth century

harp . . . lute: these stand for epic and erotic poetry, associated with Homer and Anacreon respectively

Islands of the Blest: mythical islands in the Atlantic, the reputed dwelling-place of the brave and the righteous after death

Marathon: the battlefield in northern Attica, where a small force from Athens and Plataea repulsed the first Persian attempt at invasion in 490BC

A king . . . Salamis: Xerxes, the Persian king is said to have set up a throne overlooking the bay of Salamis: there he witnessed the defeat of the Persian armada by the Greeks in 480BC

Thermopylae: in 480BC a force of three hundred Spartans held the pass of Thermopylae in Thessaly against the entire Persian army, but they were finally betrayed and annihilated

Scio's vine: Chios, besides its Homeric connection, was famous for its wine

Pyrrhic dance: an ancient war dance, performed in armour, named after its creator, Pyrrhicus

Pyrrhic phalanx: the Macedonian infantry formation used by Pyrrhus, king of Epirus (318–272BC), a brilliant commander who invaded Italy and won several battles against the Romans

Cadmus: a legendary king of Thebes, said to have introduced the alphabet into Greece

Polycrates:	ruler of Samos in the sixth century BC. The 'tyrants' of this period were self-appointed rulers who had seized power, but many gave patronage to art and letters. Anacreon was one of the beneficiaries
Miltiades:	an Athenian who was sent to his city's colony of the Chersonese (the peninsula of the Dardanelles) in the sixth century BC and made himself ruler of the region. When the first Persian expedition invaded Thrace in 492BC, Miltiades fled to Athens and was impeached for 'tyranny', but later commanded the victorious army at Marathon
Suli's rock:	the mountain of Suli in north-western Epirus was the home of a small community of Albanian Christians, famous for their military prowess. Between 1790 and 1802 they resisted attack from Ali Pasha, and when finally starved out, took refuge in Corfu
Parga's shore:	Parga, a small port on the coast of Epirus, which after many years of independence was ceded to Ali Pasha in 1815. Rather than submit to Ali's rule, the people dug up and burned the bones of their ancestors before fleeing en masse to Corfu
Doric mothers:	the mothers of the Spartans, the military élite of all the Greek city states
Heracleidan blood:	the kings of Sparta claimed descent from Heracles (Hercules)
the Franks:	the name Franks in modern Greek refers not specifically to the French, but to any Western European nation. The allusion could be to the Russians, who failed to support the Greek rising of 1770, or to the British who handed over Parga to Ali Pasha in 1815
Sunium's marbled steep:	a reference to the ruins of the temple of Poseidon on Cape Sunium in southern Attica. The temple was a well-known landmark for shipping

---

Don Juan: The Dedication

This was not published in Byron's lifetime: for the context in which it was written, see the commentary on *The Vision of Judgment* (p. 43). Byron addresses Robert Southey (1774–1843) both as Poet Laureate and as a member of the Lake school of poets, whom he accuses of trying to monopolise poetical honours. He also charges 'The Lakers' with having sacrificed their youthful idealism for material rewards, and prophesies that posterity will judge in favour of others. He praises Milton as a noble example of a writer who never forsook his principles. Next he attacks Castlereagh as a servile orator, concerned only to perpetuate oppression and extend it outside his own country. Byron will never *feel* these chains, but cannot avoid *noticing* them even in distant Italy. Southey's only *raison d'être* is to applaud these odious policies. Since Southey claims to be an epic poet, this modern epic, *Don Juan*, is dedicated to him, though in no flattering terms.

NOTES AND GLOSSARY:

Epic Renegade: Epic because of his pretensions to write long epic poems such as *The Curse of Kehama*. Renegade because, after having espoused liberal ideals in his youth, he became a reactionary member of the Establishment

Lakers: William Wordsworth (1776–1856) was born in the Lake District, and he, Samuel Taylor Coleridge (1772–1834) and Southey all later settled there. They had all in middle age moved politically far to the right

pye: a pun on the name of Henry Pye, Poet Laureate 1790–1813, Southey's predecessor, notorious for his flattery of King George III

a-dry, Bob: 'dry bob' was Regency slang for copulation without emission of semen

the dog-star: Sirius, the dog-star, is in the ascendant during late July and early August. In ancient times, this was believed to be a period when dogs (and humans) went mad. The allusion is also to Pope's *Epistle to Dr Arbuthnot*, line 3, which implies that at this season poets are especially likely to go mad

Keswick: a town in Cumbria where Coleridge and Southey lived

Excise: in 1813 Wordsworth was appointed Distributor of Stamps, a modestly paid post in the Excise Service

bays: bay leaves, the imaginary crown of the Poet Laureate

Scott, Rogers, Campbell, Moore and Crabbe: these poets were older contemporaries of Byron: he refers to them as equal, possibly superior rivals to Wordsworth and his friends

the winged steed: Pegasus, the winged horse, which in Greek mythology is the servant of the Muses, and thus associated with poetic inspiration. Byron's Muse is less ambitious and only travels on foot

meed: reward

reversion: an interest in an estate which reverts to the grantor or his heirs at the end of a given period. The sense here is that a poet who leaves it to posterity to decide his fame may find that posterity never awards it to him

Titans: the Titans in Greek mythology were the generation of gods, who fathered Zeus and the Olympians and were overthrown by them. The reference here is to the Titan Hyperion, father of the sun-god, who rises as the sun from the sea

fallen on evil days: the reference is to *Paradise Lost*, Book VII, line 24. John Milton (1608–74), though he fell upon evil days when the Stuart monarchy was restored, never forsook his principles

the Sire ... the Son: having opposed Charles I, the poet continued to oppose Charles II

the blind old man: Milton. The reference is to the Bible, I Samuel 28. King Saul, fearing the prospect of war against the Philistines, visited the witch of Endor, who called upon the ghost of Samuel to prophesy the outcome

Castlereagh: Lord Castlereagh (1769–1822), British Foreign Secretary, was intensely disliked by Byron for his support of the European monarchies of the period and his indifference to the cause of Italian independence

Erin's gore: Erin = Ireland. Castlereagh, when Secretary for Ireland, had been active in suppressing the Irish uprising of 1798, which was supported by French troops

Ixion grindstone's: Ixion in Greek mythology had tried to seduce Hera, the wife of Zeus, and was punished by being bound to an eternally revolving wheel. The meaning is that not even a blunder can strike a spark on the grindstone, to relieve the monotony of Castlereagh's oratory. His speeches hold out nothing but endless suffering for oppressed peoples

Eutropius: a senior official of the Emperor Arcadius (AD395–408): 'the first of his sex who dared to assume the character of a Roman general', he is cited as an example of a eunuch in high office, slavishly serving a despotic master

Italy ... State-thing: Byron's Italian friends had expected England to help liberate Italy and were outraged when Venice was placed under Austrian rule. Byron misunderstood Castlereagh's policy which was to prevent the domination of Europe by the Central Powers. This required co-operation with Austria as counterbalance to Prussia and Russia

'buff and blue': the colours of the Whig party

Apostasy . . . Julian: the reference is to the Roman Emperor Julian (AD360–3), named the Apostate, because he tried to turn the Empire from Christian back to pagan worship

---

Don Juan: Canto I

An epic must have a hero, but although many contemporaries have won momentary fame, the age has decided against them, and so the poet finally settles for Don Juan. But he insists, contrary to tradition, on beginning at the beginning, and so describes Juan's birthplace of Seville and his parentage. His mother, Donna Inez, is a blue-stocking, learned in literature, science and mathematics, pious, so perfect that 'her guardian angel had given up'. (Her personality is sketched as a recognisable caricature of Byron's wife.) Her husband, Don José, does not share these tastes, but 'chose to go where'er he had a mind' and the two live in respectable disharmony. Inez opens her husband's books and papers, and tries to prove him mad (another Byronic parallel); finally their quarrels are ended by José's death, leaving Juan as his heir and Inez as his guardian. Inez strives to bring up her son as a paragon of virtue, learning and manly sports, and keeps him in a state of priggish innocence. Thus Juan grows up, over-protected and supervised by tutors to the age of sixteen.

Inez's close friend, Julia, is a dazzling beauty of twenty-three, married to the fifty-year-old Alfonso. The two women have little in common, but, according to rumour Alfonso and Inez have been lovers, and Inez has befriended Julia to camouflage the affair. Julia has seen Juan grow up: then suddenly finds his company as an adolescent embarrassing. At first she decides to stop seeing him, then believes a platonic relationship might be possible – or her husband might die. Juan is mystified by the transformation within himself. He spends hours communing with nature, but has no idea what he really wants. Julia observes his distraction; Inez apparently does not. But her indifference may be calculated, its object either to complete Juan's education, or to discredit Julia and regain Alfonso's affections. The sixth of June is the crucial day. Sitting in the garden, Julia's hand touches Juan's, he kisses her, she struggles with herself, and, whispering 'I will ne'er consent', consents.

Five months pass. Juan and Julia have become lovers. Reflecting on the pleasures of life, material and spiritual, Byron concludes that first and passionate love exceeds all others. One night, when the lovers are in bed together, Julia's maid announces in panic that Alfonso is at the door. Julia pretends to be outraged and challenges him to search her room, which he does, without result. Reproaching him she lists all the admirers she has rejected, invites him to take a legal statement and dissolves into tears. Alfonso withdraws discomfited. Juan is brought out of hiding and hustled into a closet. Alfonso returns, apologises, then sees a man's pair of shoes and dashes for his sword. Juan tussles with him momentarily and escapes.

In the sequel Alfonso sues for divorce, Inez packs off Juan abroad 'to mend his former morals and get new', while Julia is sent to a convent from which she writes a farewell letter to Juan. She ponders on how men's love differs from women's and avows that she still loves him. In a coda Byron discusses the nature of epic, claims that his is unique in presenting a true story, and defends its moral. Reviewing his life at thirty, he announces that he has left behind love and ambition and become philosophical. He gives thanks that matters are no worse, and ends as he began with a jab at Southey.

NOTES AND GLOSSARY:

Difficile est . . .: from *The Art of Poetry*. The sense of the epigraph is 'It is difficult to treat in one's own way what is common knowledge'

the pantomime: the legend of Don Juan became well known in England through Thomas Shadwell's (c.1642–92) play *The Libertine* which was adapted to pantomime and was popular in the London theatre of Byron's time

Vernon . . . the poet runs through a succession of generals, admirals and politicians as candidates for the role of hero in his epic. Admiral Vernon (1684–1757) captured Portobello from Spain; the Duke of Cumberland (1721–65) fought at Fontenoy, Dettingen, and Culloden (1745) where he defeated the army of Bonnie Prince Charlie; Admiral Hawke (1705–81) won at Quiberon Bay (1759); General Wolfe (1727–59) captured Quebec (1759); Ferdinand, Duke of Brunswick (1735–1806) fought at Minden (1759); the Marquis of Granby (1720–70) was a cavalry commander at Minden and later Commander in-Chief; General Burgoyne (1723–92) defeated the American rebels at Germanstown (1777), but surrendered at Saratoga (1777); Admiral Keppel (1725–86) captured Havana (1762); Admiral

Howe (1724–99) defeated the French at Cape St Vincent (1797); Arthur Wellesley (1769–1852) became the Duke of Wellington

Banquo's monarchs: in Shakespeare's *Macbeth* (IV.1) the king consults the witches to discover whether Banquo's issue shall ever reign in Scotland. He is shown a vision of eight kings followed by Banquo

'nine farrow': the brew mixed by the witches to weave their spell included the blood of a sow which had eaten her nine farrow (piglets)

Dumourier: or Dumouriez, French military commander who defeated the Austrians at Jemappes (1792). He later fled to England

Barnave...: politicians and intellectuals of the early years of the French Revolution: many of them were executed between 1792 and 1794

Joubert...: French military commanders in the early years of the Revolutionary and Napoleonic wars

Duncan...: British admirals of the same period

'in medias res': into the middle of the story: that is, *The Iliad* does not begin with the seduction of Helen, but in the middle of the siege of Troy

the heroic turnpike road: just as the traveller had to pay a toll to go through the turnpike, so Horace makes this approach compulsory for the heroic effect

Hidalgo: a member of the lower Spanish nobility

Calderon... Lopé: classic dramatists of the golden age of Spanish literature in the sixteenth and seventeenth centuries

Feinagle: Gregor von Feinagle was a contemporary inventor of a system of mnemonic aids

mathematical: an allusion to Byron's wife, who was an excellent mathematician

Attic: Athenian: the Greek spoken and written in ancient Athens was regarded as the purest and most literary of Greek dialects

to govern d—n: grammatically 'to govern' means to have a noun depending on it. Here the entire stanza is a mockery of pedantic learning

Romilly: an eminent lawyer who had advised Byron's wife and her family and so was especially disliked by the poet

Edgeworth...: Maria Edgeworth (1769–1849) wrote novels on Irish life and a number of didactic works. Mrs Trimmer (1741–1810) was a popular author of improving books. 'Coeleb's Wife' was the title of a novel by Hannah More (1745–1833), another edifying writer

Harrison ...: John Harrison (1693–1776), a famous clockmaker

Macassar: Macassar oil was a dressing for the hair used to make it smooth and shiny

her loving lord was *mad*: an allusion to Annabella's attempts to prove that Byron was mad

'*malus animus*': a malicious intention

Numa Pompilius: a legendary king of Rome, famous for his wisdom

Doctors' Commons: the part of the Law Courts which dealt with matrimonial cases

Ovid: the famous Roman poet (43BC–AD17), author of *The Art of Love* and many narrative poems was banished from the Emperor Augustus's court on charges of immorality

Anacreon: a lyric poet of Teos in Ionia (563–478BC), well known for his verses in praise of love and of wine

Catullus: one of the finest love poets in Latin literature (87–54BC)

Sappho: another great writer of erotic poetry who lived in Mitylene (*c*.600BC)

Longinus: a Greek literary critic of the second century AD, author of the treatise *On The Sublime*

Virgil: the greatest of Roman poets (70–19BC), author of *The Aeneid* and of pastoral poetry. The poem on Corydon referred to here describes the love of two young shepherds

Lucretius: Roman poet (96–55BC), author of the great scientific and philosophical poem *On The Nature of Things*

Juvenal: the leading Roman satirist of his age (AD60–130)

Martial: a native of Spain (AD40–104), who settled in Rome and wrote witty epigrammatic and erotic verse

Missal: a book containing the prayers for the Masses for a complete year

St Jerome: a Dalmatian Christian (AD340–420), best known as the author of *The Vulgate*, the Latin version of the Scriptures

Chrysostom: St John Chrysostom, a Greek Father of the Church (AD347–407), an eloquent preacher and writer who stressed the ascetic element in the Christian religion

St Augustine: (AD354–430), the author of *The City of God*: he devoted himself to pleasure in his youth, as is explained in *The Confessions*

Verbum sat:	an abbreviation of the Latin proverb, 'a word is enough to the wise'
zone:	a girdle: that of Venus was held in Greek mythology to possess magical properties
Boabdil:	a corruption of the name Abu Abdallah, the last Moorish king of Granada: the province was regained by the Spaniards in the 1480s
mi vien in mente:	(*Italian*) 'it comes into my mind'
St Anthony:	the first Christian monk (*c.* AD250–350). He lived in Egypt and was renowned for his strength in resisting the temptations of the flesh
mulct:	a fine
Forgot . . . carriage:	had an affair with Don Alfonso
Armida:	a beautiful enchantress: one of the principal characters in Torquato Tasso's (1544–95) epic *Jerusalem Delivered*
Tarquin:	Lucius Tarquinius, the last Etruscan king of Rome, surnamed the Proud: cited here as an example of a man not to be frightened easily
mail of proof:	armour of proved strength
mole:	breakwater
inter nos:	between ourselves
Miss Medea:	the heroine of one of Ovid's tales and of Euripides's tragedy: the daughter of the king of Colchis, she fell in love with Jason when he came to find the Golden Fleece and eloped with him: cited here as one who feels powerful instinctual emotions
a harem for a grot:	a harem instead of a hermit's cave
'Oh Love . . .':	quotation from Thomas Campbell's (1777–1844) narrative poem 'Gertrude of Wyoming' (1809)
transport:	rapture
So that their plan:	assuming that their plan . . .
Boscan . . .:	Juan Boscan (1490–1542) and Garcilasso de la Vega (1503–36) were lyric poets of the Renaissance period in Spanish literature
March has its hares:	hares were popularly believed to run mad in March
post-house:	inn where horses could be changed
post-obits:	events or actions which take place after the death of the interested party
houri:	a beautiful woman: in Muslim belief numbers of these minister to the virtuous in Paradise
Anacreon Moore:	a nickname for Thomas Moore, the Irish poet
Oh Plato!:	Byron upbraids the philosopher for his advocacy of a purely spiritual love, free of sensual desire

Xerxes:	king of Persia, who launched an unsuccessful invasion of Greece (480BC)
poetic licence:	the freedom claimed by poets to let the imagination run free or ignore strict probability
Aristotle:	the reference is to Aristotle's literary treatise *The Poetics*, and its so-called Rules, which laid down, for example, that the action of a drama should be confined to one day
Bacchanal:	adjective derived from Bacchanalia, the festival of Bacchus, the Roman god of wine
prize-money:	reward for capturing an enemy ship
ambrosial:	ambrosia was the food of the Greek gods
Prometheus:	one of the Titans, who stole the secret of fire from heaven and gave it to mankind, for which he was punished by Zeus
vaccination:	Edward Jenner (1749–1823), a pioneer of inoculation against smallpox
antithesis:	Jenner's discovery helped to save life, Congreve's to destroy it
Congreve:	Sir William Congreve (1772–1828), a pioneer of the use of the rocket as an artillery weapon
galvanism:	Luigi Galvani (1737–98), an Italian physician who experimented with the action of electricity upon the muscles of frogs: shocks administered to dead bodies resulted in muscular spasms. The experiments were later extended to human bodies
Humane Society:	The Royal Humane Society was founded in England in 1774, to restore life through artificial respiration to those apparently drowned
the great pox:	syphilis was said to have been brought from America to Europe by the sailors and explorers of the fifteenth and sixteenth centuries
lues:	venereal disease
Davy's lantern:	Sir Humphry Davy (1778–1829) invented the miner's safety lamp
Tombuctoo travels:	probably a reference to J. G. Jackson's book (1809) on Timbuctoo, the great Emporium of Western Africa, on the Niger
her husband's temples...:	to encumber with horns, the mark of the cuckold
Cortejo:	noble suitor
rout:	party with music and dancing
Count O'Reilly:	an Irish soldier of fortune who unsuccessfully attacked Algiers (1775)

Cazzani ... Nunez: imaginary names for Julia's past admirers

should be fee'd: should incur legal expenses

myrmidons: attendants

Achates: the faithful companion of Aeneas in Virgil's epic *The Aeneid*

Job's wife: see the Bible, Job 2:10

'*posse comitatus*': company of able-bodied men

'*hiatus*': inconsistency in Alfonso's story

maudlin Clarence: the Duke of Clarence, younger brother of King Richard III, was reputedly drowned for suspected treason in a cask of Malmsey wine

Hebrew Chronicle: see the Bible, I Kings 1

'*rigmarole*': a long and complicated statement

Tartar: member of the Mongolian tribe which overran Europe in the thirteenth century: here the word signifies a formidable fighter

Joseph: for the story of Joseph and Potiphar's wife, see the Bible, Genesis 39

nonsuit: order the dismissal of a lawsuit

Gurney: W. B. Gurney was official shorthand writer to the Houses of Parliament and reported trials and speeches all over Britain in Byron's time

the Vandals: a Germanic tribe which invaded France and Spain in the fourth century AD and migrated to North Africa in the fifth

mart: market

***Elle vous suit partout*:** it follows you everywhere

a feather: to win the public's favour is an achievement for an author

in training: in prospect

***Vade Mecum*:** handbook

'the Blues': 'Blue' is an abbreviation for 'Blue Stocking', a woman having or affecting literary tastes. The allusion to 'false witness' may refer to Lady Caroline Lamb and her novel *Glenarvon* which contained a fictional portrait of Byron

Longinus: see note on p. 38

kiss the rod: accept punishment humbly

my Grandmother's Review: an elaborate joke on Byron's part. When *Don Juan* first appeared anonymously, the *British Review* argued in its notice that the poem could not be Byron's, since no English nobleman would stoop to alleging an editor's acceptance of a bribe. Byron wrote to the editor under a pseudonym, professing

	ignorance of the author of *Don Juan* and absolving the editor of any suspicion of bribery
Edinburgh Review ... Quarterly:	two of the leading literary journals of the day
Non ego ...:	'I should not have borne this in my hot youth when Plancus was consul': the quotation is paraphrased in the last two lines of the stanza
the Brenta:	the canal in the countryside near Venice where Byron rented a summer villa
peruke:	wig
Friar Bacon:	Roger Bacon, the philosopher, (*c.*1214–1300) was credited with magical powers and with having fashioned a brazen (brass) head which could prophesy. According to Robert Greene's play *Friar Bacon and Friar Bungay*, the head was to speak, but if they did not hear all its words, the effort would be in vain. After staying awake for three weeks, Bacon was relieved by his servant and fell asleep. The head then uttered 'Time is': the servant was afraid to wake his master for so little and let him sleep. The head then continued 'Time was', and 'Time's past', and then fell and was shattered
Cheops:	King Cheops (*fl.* about 3700BC) built the Great Pyramid near Gizeh
'Go, little book':	this quotation, skilfully placed for a final gibe, is taken from Southey's absurd *The Lay of the Laureate*

The Vision of Judgment (1821)

St Peter waits at the gate of Heaven for admissions. Because of events in France, the number of candidates has shrunk of late, while the traffic for Hell has greatly increased. The angels are under-employed, save for the recording angel registering human sins, who has needed extra staff. George III has just died. His funeral was celebrated with great pomp, though little real concern on earth, but in Heaven it creates more stir. To claim the king for damnation, Satan makes one of his regular visits to St Peter, and St Michael arrives for the defence. Satan outlines the prosecution's case. George governed through favourites, he tried to suppress the natural aspirations to freedom of the American and French peoples. He possessed some domestic virtues, but he and his successors elsewhere have consolidated their hold upon absolute rule. He adopted a bigoted attitude towards Catholic emancipation. This revelation shocks St Peter, who refuses to admit the king: Michael strives to lower the temperature and calls upon Satan to produce his witnesses. These swarm in from all quarters like a cloud of locusts. Michael protests that a few persons of superior quality will be enough, whereupon Satan calls two famous opponents of the king's administration, John Wilkes (1727–97) and the anonymous pamphleteer Junius, but their evidence proves inconclusive.

Lastly the devil Asmodeus appears, dragging Southey whom he accuses of distorting both history and the Bible. Southey's latest poem, *A Vision of Judgment*, declares Asmodeus, anticipates 'the very business you are here upon'. Southey begins to read *A Vision* aloud, but this is received with such disgust that the poet is reduced to defending himself in prose. He pleads that he meant no harm in writing: he has only toiled to earn his bread. To do this he first upheld regicide and universal equality, then attacked them: he has written defending war and pacifism, attacked reviewers and been one himself, written a biography of Wesley and now proposes one of Satan, or, failing that, of St Michael. Here he tries again to read from *A Vision*, but after three lines, the audience departs, some to Heaven, some to Hell. St Peter hurls him down into the infernal lake, but Southey, like a rotting corpse, floats to the surface. Amid the confusion, King George quietly slips into Heaven and is heard practising the hundredth psalm.

COMMENTARY: The publication of *The Vision of Judgment* marked the climax of one of the bitterest feuds in English letters, the quarrel between Byron and Southey. Byron had long disliked Southey, seeing him as a political reactionary, a smug and obsequious Poet Laureate, and the least gifted of the Lake poets. In 1817 Southey visited Switzerland and was said to have circulated scandalous stories concerning Byron's visit a year before: as the story reached Byron, Southey had spoken of 'a league of incest' in which Shelley and Byron took part with Mary Godwin and Claire Claremont.

In 1819 the first two cantos of *Don Juan* were published anonymously. The *Dedication* attacking Southey did not appear, but Southey heard of it. In January 1819 King George III died, and a year later Southey published *A Vision of Judgment*, a blatantly flattering composition, which describes the reception of the old, mad king into Heaven. The preface contained a thinly veiled attack upon *Don Juan* and its author, 'men of diseased hearts and depraved imaginations', who have set up 'what may properly be called the Satanic school.' Byron promptly began his counter-attack and finished it in September 1821. John Murray, apprehensive of another literary uproar, delayed passing the proofs and finally handed over the manuscript to Leigh Hunt's brother John. Byron's *Vision* appeared in October 1822 under the pseudonym Quevedo Redivivus (Quevedo re-born): Quevedo was a seventeenth-century Spanish poet, the author of a number of visionary writings.

Hunt was prosecuted by the Crown for publishing *The Vision*, and fined in July 1824, a few days after Byron had been buried in England.

NOTES AND GLOSSARY:

the Gallic era: the French Revolution began in 1789

another way: to Hell, not to Heaven

reversion: an interest in an estate that reverts, at the end of a period or a life to the grantor; the meaning here is that after death both generals, Napoleon and Wellington, would revert to the possession of Satan

In the first year: George III died in 1819: in the same year various national revolts broke out in southern Europe

Saint John's . . . beast: see the Bible, Revelations 13

One half as mad: the king had suffered for many years from blindness and attacks of insanity

unnatural balsams: the king's body had been embalmed

German will: a pun upon the two meanings, (i) germane = relevant, (ii) German = the king's nationality

proctor: an agent employed to conduct another's case in court

constancy: George III's marriage was exceptionally stable, George IV's was the opposite. He married Princess Caroline of Brunswick in 1795, was separated in 1796, and the divorce proceedings occasioned a political and public scandal in 1820, the year before *The Vision* appeared

save the like: a pun upon the two meanings of save: (i) protect, (ii) do without, the king being God's representative on earth

circumscribing . . .: Byron claims to be tolerant by nature: he wonders whether he is alone is trying to reduce the fearful danger of eternal hell fire

all save England's church: a reference to the fact that the Church of England is Established, that is, recognised as a national institution

the last we saw here: Louis XVI, guillotined in 1793

Paul – the parvenu: as a belated convert to Christianity, Paul is regarded with some jealousy by Peter

ichor: in Greek mythology the fluid running in the veins of the gods

Orion's belt: the three stars grouped in the centre of the constellation known as Orion (The Hunter)

manes: (*Latin*) spirits of the dead

Aurora borealis: the moving bands of light seen in the sky in the polar regions

Captain Parry's crew: in 1819–20 Edward Parry made a voyage which threw new light on the age-old question of the existence of a North-West Passage

Joanna Southcote: a religious fanatic (1750–1814) who left behind her a box, which she claimed would be found to contain momentous revelations when opened

champ clos: literally *closed field*, a chosen battleground

eastern thresholds: a reference to the Eastern custom of holding courts of law outside a palace

quit-rent: originally a rent paid by a freeholder to his feudal lord which released the former from certain services

a minion: a servile favourite: the reference is to Lord Bute, Prime Minister 1761–3, appointed by the king soon after his accession to the throne

So that . . .: the sense is 'If they ever uttered'

Apicius . . . anchorite's: Apicius was a Roman notorious for his passion for food. The sense is that it is more impressive to show restraint in the company of an Apicius than in that of a hermit

the primitive: believers in the Roman Catholic faith

Guelph: originally in Italian history the Guelphs were the opponents of the Holy Roman Emperor Frederick I, and the Ghibellines his supporters against the Papacy: in Florence the Ghibellines were identified with the republican faction, and so in Regency slang Guelph signified reactionary sympathies. Both names are German in origin, hence a further association of Guelph with George III

Cerberus: the three-headed dog which in Greek mythology guards the entry to the underworld

Bedlam bigot: bigoted madman. Bedlam was the principal lunatic asylum in London

damn'd away his eyes: 'damn your eyes!' is a traditional English imprecation

Paddy brogued: an Irishman said

Otaheite: Tahiti

Wilkes: John Wilkes, an MP well known for the immorality of his private life and his outspoken criticism of the king's supporters. He founded the *North Briton*, a journal which attacked Bute's government

Grafton: Duke of Grafton, Prime Minister 1767–70

Charon's ferry: in Greek mythology Charon was the boatman who ferried the dead across the river Styx into the underworld

Fox's lard: William Pitt (1759–1806) was leader of the Tory party and Prime Minister, 1783–1801. Fox, the leader of the Opposition, was his most eloquent critic. Fox was greatly overweight: Pitt is pictured as impaled on a spit in Hell, being basted with lard from Fox

gagg'd: a reference to Pitt's wartime legislation restricting the freedom of the press

Junius: the anonymous author of a series of pamphlets attacking the government in the years 1769–72. His identity was never established

epistolary 'Iron Mask': epistolary because the pamphlets were entitled *The Letters of Junius*. The mask alludes to a prisoner said to have been kept in the Bastille during the reign of Louis XIV, whose face was concealed

Malaprop ... Burke ... Tooke ... Francis: Mrs Malaprop, a character in Richard Brinsley Sheridan's (1751–1816) play *The Rivals* (1775), who habitually mis-spells long words and reveals her ignorance in the attempt to show her learning. Edmund Burke (1729–97), a prominent orator and thinker of the Tory party. Horne Tooke (1736–1812) was well known both as a philologist and a radical in politics. Sir Philip Francis (1740–1818), a writer on politics credited by some with the authorship of *The Letters of Junius*

'What I have written': in the preceding stanza Byron invokes the reader's sympathy for Junius as a patriot. But 'What I have written ...' was also said by Pontius Pilate in justification of his decision to hand over Christ to the Jews

'Nominis Umbra' ...: the reference is to a phrase from Lucan's (AD39–65) Latin epic poem *Pharsalia*, II.135 – 'there stands the shadow of a glorious name'

Franklin: Benjamin Franklin (1706–90) represented the American colonies and later the United States for many years as a diplomat and political emissary in England and Europe

Asmodeus: the principal character in Le Sage's novel *The Lame Devil*. He lifts the roofs off private houses to reveal what is happening inside: thus in stanza 86 he sees Southey at work and transports him to the celestial trial

ass ... like Balaam's: the prophet Balaam's ass, when beaten by its master, was divinely prompted to speak. In this way

	Balaam received God's message. See the Bible, Numbers 22
spavin'd:	a veterinary term applied to a horse's leg, meaning swollen and limping
dactyls:	dactyl is a foot of three syllables, one long followed by two short syllables, used in a hexameter
***Non Di, non homines*:**	this quotation from Horace's *Art of Poetry* has been abbreviated. The sense, in context, is 'Neither gods nor men nor booksellers have tolerated second-rate poets'
***Pye*:**	Henry James Pye was Southey's predecessor as Poet Laureate. See *Dedication* to *Don Juan*, stanza 1
poetic felony '*de se*':	*felo de se* is the legal term for the criminal offence of committing or attempting to commit suicide
'Wat Tyler' . . .:	titles of Southey's works
pantisocracy:	a community in which all are equal and share in government. In 1794 Southey had planned to emigrate with Coleridge and join such a community in America
King Alfonso:	Alfonso X (1252–82), king of Castile, was named the Wise and the Astronomer. Speaking of the Ptolemaic system of cosmology he said that had he been consulted at the creation of the world, he could have saved the Creator some absurdities
'melodious twang':	a quotation from the antiquary John Aubrey (1626–97) who in his *Lives* describes a ghost as vanishing 'with a melodious twang'
Phaeton:	the son of Helios, the sun-god. In Greek legend the youth begged his father to let him drive the chariot of the sun across the sky. He lost control and was killed
corrupted things:	a drowned body, after corruption sets in, floats to the surface of the water
the hundredth psalm:	the psalm exhorts man to praise God cheerfully. The king was fond of music, and in this ironic conclusion Byron sees the man who had caused all the fuss slipping into Heaven unnoticed

---

The Island   (1823)

This tale, based on the historical narrative of the mutiny on HMS *Bounty*, consists of four Cantos. The extract selected here contains eighty-four lines from Canto III. The rest of the plot is summarised so as to place this passage in context.

Canto I: As the *Bounty* sails through a calm sea at dawn, the mutiny breaks out. The unsuspecting Bligh and the loyal members of the crew are forced into a long-boat and cast adrift. The vessels part, those in the boat to suffer fearful hardships before rescue, the mutineers to return to the island paradise of Tahiti, which is still uncorrupted by the vices of civilisation.

Canto II: The first three sections describing the island's landscape and its inhabitants are based on folksongs from Marriner's book on the Tonga Islands. Neuha, the young heroine, 'the sunflower of the island's daughters' is described, together with her husband Torquil, who comes of Hebridean stock. In Torquil Byron sees an idealised picture of his own Scottish boyhood, and recalls how he, a northerner, was likewise captivated by the south, so that through his eyes 'Lochnagar looked o'er Troy'. The young couple's happiness seems unclouded, but one of the mutineers interrupts their idyll with news of the arrival of a British warship: he summons Torquil to help oppose the landing.

Canto III: The unequal struggle soon ends and the mutineers are hunted all over the island. The survivors gather under a huge cliff. Fletcher Christian, their leader, has no thought of surrender, but wishes Torquil to escape. Neuha arrives with a pair of canoes. She embarks with Torquil in one and Christian's party in another, just as their British pursuers approach.

Canto IV: Both canoes are chased by the British sailors and at length part company. Neuha paddles to a nearby islet, dives overboard followed by Torquil and swims underwater into a huge subterranean cave. There she had prepared a cavern within the grotto, stocked with food and fuel. Christian and his comrades land on another islet, where they die fighting to the end. The frigate sails away, and Neuha and Torquil return to their island home.

COMMENTARY: *The Island* is Byron's last poem of any considerable length: it was completed at Genoa four months before he sailed for Greece. Not long before, Byron had considered emigrating to South America, and *The Island*, alone among the *Tales* is pervaded by the theme of escape. Tooboonai is seen as a primitive paradise which embodies the eighteenth-century dream of the superiority of the noble uncorrupted savage to civilised European man.

The poem has two main sources – Captain Bligh's *Narrative of the Mutiny on the Bounty* and William Marriner's *Account of the Natives of the Tonga Islands*. Byron accepts, surprisingly, Bligh's version of his own innocence and the mutineers' guilt. He draws upon Marriner for local colour, but many of the details he gives, both historical and geographical, are imaginary. In reality the *Bounty* arrived in Tahiti in October 1788 and sailed for home in April 1789: the mutiny broke out three weeks later. Bligh was cast adrift with eighteen men, the remaining twenty-four staying with Fletcher Christian. The *Bounty* then sailed to Tooboonai, leaving for Tahiti in June: she returned to Tooboonai later that month and finally to Tahiti in September, when sixteen of the mutineers stayed ashore. Christian left Tahiti taking with him the remaining eight of the mutineers and some Tahitian men and women and settled on the then uninhabited Pitcairn Island. There they lived undiscovered until 1808, by which date only one of the mutineers was still alive: their descendants still inhabit the island. Meanwhile Bligh and his crew had been rescued, and in 1790 the frigate *Pandora* was despatched to arrest the mutineers. Fourteen of the sixteen were taken prisoner and the ten who survived the voyage back from Tahiti were court-martialled in England.

NOTES AND GLOSSARY:

as he wings a tomb: as the cannon causes a tomb, that is, death, to fly through the air

Once renegades: once they had become renegades from their native land through the act of mutiny

deem'd their lot/Not pardon'd: their hope had been not that they would be pardoned, but forgotten and not pursued

Their new allies: the natives of the island

sulphury charm: the gunpowder and modern weapons carried by the *Pandora*

Till *now*, when she: a topical reference to the Greek War of Independence which had begun in 1821

Part 3

Commentary

Literary background

Byron was the eldest of the 'second wave' of the English Romantic poets.
The generation of Wordsworth and Coleridge was in its teens when the
French Revolution began, and at first they hailed it with joy and hope,
emotions which later gave way to disillusion, fear and an upsurge of
patriotism. For Byron, Shelley and Keats the revolutionary atmosphere
had already passed into history, and they grew up in the era of the
Napoleonic wars, in times of national peril, of momentous battles such
as Trafalgar and Waterloo, in a world dominated by absolute rulers,
first by Napoleon, later by the restored Bourbons and the Holy Alliance.
Thus their political or social idealism was focused upon the sufferings of
the industrial poor at home, or of oppressed nations abroad, Italians,
Spaniards, Greeks. Wordsworth had written of humble and rustic
subjects because there 'the essential conditions of the heart find a better
soil in which to flourish', and his and Coleridge's poems are deeply
rooted in the pieties of English country life. The poetry of Byron, Shelley
and Keats, like that of the European Romantics, moves into wider
realms of mythology, history or dream, not only in its physical or
spiritual location, but in its handling of ideological argument, ethical
conflict or aesthetic ideals.

Byron, however, also stands apart from the 'second wave': there are
more important differences between his poetry and that of Keats and
Shelley than there are resemblances. The other major Romantic poets
made high claims for the value of poetry and lived the lives of dedicated
artists. Byron, by contrast, produced no manifesto comparable to
Wordsworth's Preface to *Lyrical Ballads* or Shelley's *Defence of Poetry*,
nor could he analyse his own poetic practice with the acumen of Keats:
indeed he wrote very little on poetic theory until 1821 (his letters
attacking Bowles's criticisms of Pope). In his London years he declared
that he did not rate poets or poetry high in the scale of intellect, and he
described the poetic process as a kind of personal therapy. 'If I don't
write to empty my mind, I go mad .... Poetry is the lava of the
imagination which prevents an earthquake', and certainly much of the
early poetry which made him famous, such as the *Turkish Tales*, reflects
this view of composition. His Journal for the last week of November
1813 is particularly relevant: 'Who would write who had anything better
to do? .... Actions, actions, I say, and not writing, least of all rhyme.'

Byron's opinion of writers in general was much influenced by his social position, though paradoxical even from that viewpoint. He desired passionately to be widely read, but not to be classed as a professional writer. His ideal was the combination of writer and man of action, such as the Greek tragedian Aeschylus and the Spanish novelist Cervantes, who saw military service, not the type of writer who patiently perfects his texts year by year in semi-monastic seclusion. He thought it indispensable for the poet to possess a wide experience of life

> Men of the world, who know the World like Men,
> And think of something else besides the pen

Here he thought the Lake poets ill-equipped. 'They know nothing of the world, and what is poetry but the reflection of the world? What sympathy have these people with the spirit of this stirring age? Southey ought to have been a parish-clerk and Wordsworth a man mid-wife. I doubt if either of them ever got drunk.' The writers whose company Byron most enjoyed – Sheridan, Scott, Moore and the critic Gifford, all (with the notable exception of Shelley) displayed a sceptical and worldly-wise strain in their personalities, and were far removed from the contemporary type of Romantic genius.

Behind this paradox of desiring literary fame, yet despising the full-time 'scribbler', lies a deeper paradox. Byron's social eminence allowed him to see himself as potentially capable of (and hence responsible for) swaying opinion and inducing political change, a prospect beyond the reach of other Romantic poets or artists. This fact helps to explain his attachment to the Augustan era, in which the writer, as a man of position, could and did influence cultural and spiritual standards. It also places Byron in an exceptional situation *vis-à-vis* the Romantic movement, since he was less exposed than his contemporaries to a sense of isolation from their public and of helplessness to implement their ideals. This said, Byron probably owed more to his early literary success than he cared to admit. 'Until his talents became known,' Lord Holland, the Whig leader wrote, 'Byron did not move in good society, and but for his talents might never have done so.' After Byron left England, he again became to some extent dependent on his poetic fame: at least he could hardly have wielded the influence he did in Italy and Greece had he been no more than an expatriate English milord.

Byron's taste in literature remained, in theory at least, consistently conservative. In *English Bards* he followed the example of recent satirists and, claiming to defend the traditional Augustan virtues of clarity and good sense, attacked most of the innovators of the day. He criticised Wordsworth for his prosaic diction and choice of lowly subjects, Coleridge for his obscurity, Southey for his inflated epics, Scott for his antiquarian romances in verse, 'Monk' Lewis for his Gothic horror-fiction. Ten years later he criticised the so-called 'Cockney' school of Hunt and Keats, whose writing he at first regarded as cheap fantasy, constructed out of inferior materials.

To understand this judgment, we need to consider Byron's view of the imagination. Byron disagreed with the Wordsworthian and Coleridgean view of the imagination as the supreme source of poetic creation. He contended that the significance of an experience, the impact of a personality, event or object cannot be apprehended solely from the viewpoint of the individual imagination: the experience exists *in context*, and the context is larger than our individual awareness. So if we insist on the primacy of the imagination, we become increasingly self-absorbed. Such self-absorption is likely to produce the qualities Byron most disliked in Romantic writing, the tendency to withdraw into a private world, a one-to-one relationship towards the reader: with the Lake poets he considered that this led to oracular, grandiose, over-enthusiastic accounts of experience. Here lies the root of Byron's antagonism to the poetry of his major Romantic contemporaries: they, as he saw it, placed the highest value on the intensity of the individual vision. 'In my mind', Byron wrote, 'the highest of all poetry is ethical poetry, as the highest of all earthly objects must be moral truth ... he who can reconcile truth and wisdom is the only true poet in its real sense.' The other Romantics would not have disputed the supreme importance of the quest for truth: the disagreement may now appear to us to have concerned means rather than ends. To sum up, Byron chose to regard life as the measure of imagination, not *vice versa*, and his insight functioned at its best on a social and analytical plane.

As it happened, Byron's early work, especially the *Turkish Tales* produced examples of strained and inflated writing quite as bad as anything he had criticised in his contemporaries. However the *Tales* launched him on a tide of commercial and international success which lasted the rest of his life. His publisher clamoured for new work, and in his correspondence we move in a world of literary acclaim, social eminence and international notoriety, a public sphere which is entirely different from the circumstances of the other English Romantics.

Byron's defence of Augustan literature reflects his preference for writing which offers truth to life and is based on a wide knowledge of the world. But in many other respects it was an unsuitable model for him to emulate. For all his admiration of Pope's style, he did not possess the convictions, the decorum, nor the fineness of judgment which went to make up that style. Pope writes from a secure platform of social, ethical and cultural values: his satire censures lapses from those standards, and even at his most insulting, he does not depart from strict decorum. Byron is writing in an age which has lost such firm footholds, and his satire is based on irreverence and derision. Compared with the subtly directed thrusts of Pope's literary criticisms, *English Bards* is knockabout comedy. And when, as in *The Vision of Judgment*, Byron is writing from an aristocratic standpoint, he feels free, whether attacking the king or the commoner, to hit below the belt. In other words Pope, upholding a high standard, condemns all who fall below it: Byron, when he attacks oppression or hypocrisy, appeals to a common humanity, so much as to say, 'you are no better than the worst of us'. As a literary form the rhyming couplet, the perfect medium for Augustan literature, did not suit Byron because he lacked the capacity for sustained ideological exposition or satirical argument. Even his best satirical poem, *The Vision of Judgment*, is fashioned in narrative rather than argumentative form. Byron found *his* ideal medium when he hit upon the *ottava rima* stanza, which enabled him to present his own satirical vision in its peculiarly discursive form and to write in his natural tone and vocabulary.

Narrative poems

Between the triumph of *Childe Harold* (1812) and the tragedy of his exile (1816), Byron's writing, apart from *Hebrew Melodies*, was dominated by his experiments in narrative poetry – the five *Turkish Tales* and *Parisina*. Several reasons may explain why his poetic impulse was directed towards this form. The self-protective role of literary satirist which he had assumed in *English Bards* after the criticisms of *Hours of Idleness* offered only a narrow scope for his gifts: he was dissatisfied with the satire and withdrew it in 1812. He was encouraged by Murray to exploit the success of *Childe Harold*, and there were experiences fresh in his memory which he had not used in that poem. Thus the plot of *The Giaour* originated from an episode in Athens when Byron had rescued a girl condemned to be drowned in a sack, the Ottoman punishment for infidelity. Throughout his years in London Byron continued to draw inspiration from his Near Eastern travels: it was moreover a literary territory in which none of his contemporaries could rival him.

At this date other private influences, less easy to assess, may also have been at work. His entangled personal relationships drove him from time to time to 'empty his mind' by writing. This impetus inspired especially *The Giaour*, *The Bride of Abydos*, and *The Corsair*, which were composed between late 1812 and 1814, the last two each in a few days. *The Bride* and *Parisina* skirt the topic of incest. The heroines of the other stories present variations of the image of a girl with whose death, it is implied, the author feels himself involved. In each tale the passion of love is depicted as an irresistible force, destructive to those who experience it. Finally, this was a time when Byron, originally ambitious for an active public career as a champion of reform, was becoming disillusioned with the political scene, and with his own capacities as a performer on it. 'All I can do is make my life an amusement', he wrote in his *Journal* in November 1813. The Byronic hero whom he invented may have supplied him with fantasies of action to compensate for his feelings of disappointment and self-betrayal in the political sphere.

The verse tale was a form which attracted all the English Romantics, and Coleridge and Keats handle it with a degree of artistry which often leaves Byron far behind. *Christabel* and *The Eve of St Agnes* possess mythical and allegorical qualities which are quite lacking in the *Turkish Tales*. Byron, who remarked that *The Bride of Abydos* was written 'standing on one foot', characteristically suggested to Coleridge concerning the eternally unfinished *Christabel*, 'surely a little effort would complete the poem'. Byron is often described as endowed beyond his contemporaries with an overwhelming energy, and this is the redeeming quality most conspicuous in his stories: some of the action in *The Giaour* and most of it in *Mazeppa* actually take place on a galloping horse. In the *Turkish Tales* the narrative impetus is strong, the settings highly coloured, the external details of scenery, customs, dress and weaponry minutely accurate. Byron prided himself on authenticity in these matters and his attention to realism helps to conceal the haste and crudity of some of the writing.

The Corsair and its sequel *Lara* offer the most ambitious portrait of the Byronic hero. His character and psychology are sketched in Canto I, sections 9–12 of *The Corsair*. He is an aristocrat and a natural leader, endowed with exceptional vitality, courage and self-control, pitiless to his enemies, tender and unswervingly constant to his love, Medora. Early in life he had suffered some unspecified injustice or misfortune, which had caused him to spurn society and seek revenge upon it

> His soul was changed, before his deeds had driven
> Him forth to war with man, and forfeit heaven.

There is much here that corresponds to Byron's image of himself, as a man of exceptional qualities who is also the victim of fate. Conrad exults in the mode of life of the corsair, which embodies the outstanding characteristic of the Byronic hero, his unconquerable resistance to subjection. In the mythology of the Romantic era, this attribute was not confined to the mortal scale, but elevated to the divine. Prometheus's defiance of Zeus and Lucifer's of God were seen as supreme examples of revolutionary rejection of absolute authority, and Byron was to treat such themes in his dramas *Manfred* and *Cain*. In the *Tales* the subject is handled at the human level. The adventurer of noble instincts such as Conrad is presented as the breed of man who is capable of upholding the heroic ideal in a contemporary world corrupted by wealth and oppression: but circumstances warp his destiny and drive him to war against society. The resemblance to the prototype of the righteous outlaw, Robin Hood, is obvious, and Byron can scarcely have been unmindful of the tradition – Newstead Abbey borders upon Sherwood Forest.

Conrad, however, even though the most fully portrayed of the heroes, remains an incomplete character. He cannot respond to Medora's attempt to change or soften his predatory attitude to the world, nor to Gulnare, who in saving his life destroys his honour and his masculinity as he sees them. The weakness of the *Tales* lies in the superficiality of the characterisation and the melodramatic nature of the action: what they lack by comparison, say, with *The Ancient Mariner* is depth of insight into human nature and human motive. Byron does not trouble to explore the sufferings which have transformed his hero's nature, nor draw the lessons of experience from these. The reader may be entertained by the dramatic turns of the plot, but it is impossible to be moved by the fate of Conrad, Lara, the Giaour and the rest.

By 1816 Byron had come to recognise these failings. In *The Prisoner of Chillon* he broke new ground, as described earlier, in writing a severely naturalistic narrative which had no connection with experiences of his own. Having just completed *Beppo*, a mock-heroic epic, he introduces a note of sardonic humour into his *Mazeppa* (1818), a tale of passion and adventure, and gives a foretaste of the method he was to employ in *Don Juan*. Mazeppa tells his story as an old soldier looking back on his first serious love affair. The youthful Mazeppa is as much a victim of his uncontrolled passions as the Giaour: the old Mazeppa describes his plight with a detachment similar to that of Byron-as-commentator chronicling the adventures of Juan. In *The Island* Byron returns to the vein of romantic fantasy, but this time the role of the hero is shared by two characters. Fletcher Christian, the leader of the *Bounty* mutineers, is a typical guilt-ridden Byronic protagonist of the 1813 model: Torquil, the innocent hero, a noble savage with an infusion of Scottish blood, harks back to the Byron of *Hours of Idleness*.

Childe Harold's Pilgrimage

Childe Harold dominates Byron's creative life in the first half of his career as *Don Juan* does in the second. Like *The Prelude* it is one of the great testaments of the Romantic sensibility. Wordsworth describes the growth of a poet's mind looking back on a series of past events. In *Childe Harold* the events unfold before our eyes. Byron chronicles his impressions moment by moment and his life changes through each Canto of the poem. The title-word *Pilgrimage* is significant. The poem represents a voyage of self-discovery. Byron's motives for going abroad were at first dissatisfaction with his life in England, a resolve to establish his independence, and a desire to savour the world in all its diversity. In this regard he travelled not only to explore the unknown but also with the Romantic impulse to seek out an unattainable ideal, a vision of the world which turns out not to exist. Thus he travelled to Greece (Canto II) in search of those sources of human greatness, the traditions of heroism and freedom established by the ancient Greeks. Still, he looked back on those two years as the most completely fulfilled period in his life. But when his expulsion from English society caused him to resume his travels, the Pilgrimage became a way of life and an act of self-restoration.

No-one has written a sonnet 'On First Looking Into Childe Harold's Pilgrimage', but the reading public of 1812 at once recognised that a new planet had appeared. This was partly because the previous ten years had been very uneventful for English poetry. Scott and Moore were the new names; apart from *Lyrical Ballads* (1798) and Wordsworth's *Poems of 1807* almost all the major works of the Romantic era appeared after 1815. The travel poem describing famous ruins and landscapes was a familiar genre, but hitherto an inert one. *Childe Harold* touched the nerve of the time: the drums of the Napoleonic wars sound subtly but insistently off-stage throughout. What immediately arrested attention was the first-hand quality of the material. Here was a new author who had actually rubbed shoulders with Oriental pashas and Albanian banditti, and could describe the glories of Greece in their living setting of natural beauty and human cruelty. And in the midst of these adventures Byron sounded a deeper note, which links Canto II to III and IV, a meditation upon man's present and past, upon the grandeur of Nature viewed amid the wreckage of empires. Besides this the poem was easy to read: it combined the warmth and directness of statement of Romantic verse with the resounding generalities of the eighteenth-century style.

Childe Harold is written in the nine-line stanza originally devised by Spenser for *The Faerie Queene*. Its distinctive features are the closely woven rhyme scheme – *ababbcbcc* – and the alexandrine, the twelve-syllable ninth line which rhymes with its predecessor and closes the stanza. The metre attracted other Romantic poets, Shelley in 'Adonais' and Keats in 'The Eve of St Agnes'. Keats's poetry displays much of the sensuous and dream-like quality of Spenser's, and so the form is well suited to the slow-moving, richly decorated stanzas of *The Eve*. Byron uses it very differently, not always with success. Eighteenth-century models such as James Thomson's (1700–48) *The Castle of Indolence* (1748) had shown that the stanza could create a wide range of effects, satirical, sentimental or grand. Such variety of tone was needed for a poem of patchwork texture, with frequent shifts of scene and mood. In the passages on the ruins of Greece and Rome Byron touches one of Edmund Spenser's (?1552–99) principal themes, 'Mutability', and here his handling of the stanza does approach the stately movement of Spenser's *The Faerie Queene*. Elsewhere Byron successfully adapts it to scenes of action, as in the Waterloo sequence (Canto III) 'Arm! Arm! it is – it is – the cannon's opening roar'. Keats and Shelley, however, use the stanza for comparatively short poems of a shapely structure. Byron uses it as a hold-all, and for this purpose it is a cumbersome measure which tends to imprison his writing in a grandiose and inflated diction and to minimise the vitality and gusto which came naturally to him: he learned to exploit these qualities to the full when he discovered the *ottava rima* stanza.

Cantos I–II

The modern reader, if he is to pass beyond the enjoyment of the famous purple passages and grasp the poem as a whole, needs to examine its structure and the differences which distinguish the Cantos. Canto I is the simplest and most resembles a versified travelogue. It gives a straightforward account of the visit to Portugal and Spain with descriptions of the landscape, the Peninsular war, the bull-fight, the revengeful nature of the Spanish people. Canto II devotes the first sixteen stanzas to the key motif, the meditation upon vanished glories and vanished creeds amid the ruins of the Acropolis. This is echoed by the brief elegy to Greek freedom (stanzas 73–6). These two contemplative passages frame the main action of the Canto, the voyage to western Greece on a British warship, and the brilliant picture of the court of Ali Pasha and the savage valour of the Albanian highlanders. The world of Ali is dramatised, as Byron was especially skilful in doing, through the lyric 'Tambourgi! Tambourgi!' (the military drummer who summons the tribesmen to battle). There follows a short description of Istanbul and a further lament on the current degradation of the once glorious Greece. After Byron's return to England, the death of his mother and of his friends, Charles Matthews and John Edleston, caused him to add four stanzas which close the Canto on a note of mourning. The phrasing of the last stanza 'Before the Chastener humbly let me bow' suggests a mood of penitence, which Byron's readers may not have taken too seriously.

Canto III

From the beginning of this Canto Byron adopts a different authorial tone. In I and II the dominant note is one of surprise and wonder: an unknown young man is visiting foreign peoples and scenes, some famous, some unfamiliar. In Canto III Byron is a travelling celebrity, writing now on public, now on private themes. On the first plane, he is describing the aftermath of the greatest political and military convulsion his contemporaries had known: his picture of the famous Brussels ball and of the field of Waterloo was created less than a year after the battle. Elsewhere he writes of Rousseau, the forerunner of the Revolution and of Napoleon, its principal actor, 'The madmen who have made men mad/By their contagion'. These are passages of high tension which are matched in vehemence by Byron's account of his own tortured state of mind. Another element which distinguishes this Canto springs from Byron's association with Shelley. Shelley communicated something of his enthusiasm for Wordsworth's poetry to Byron, and the feelings aroused in the latter by the lakes and mountains of Switzerland play an important part in the poem. Wordsworth later accused Byron of having plagiarised his feelings for natural objects and spoiled them while doing so. Yet Byron's attitude towards Nature is, and always was, clearly distinct from Wordsworth's. In Canto II he wrote

> To sit on rocks, to muse on flood and fell,
> This is not solitude: 'tis but to hold
> Converse with Nature's charms . . .

and he identified solitude with a sense of isolation from mankind, quite unconnected with his feelings concerning Nature. But in Canto III his feeling is differently explained:

> I live not in myself, but I become
> Portion of that around me, and to me
> High mountains are a feeling, but the hum
> Of human cities torture . . .

Here Byron turns to Nature to take refuge from his fellow-men: he is not, as in the earlier Canto, celebrating Nature for her own sake. Rather Nature here provides him with images of mountains, wind and water, which embody his own tempestuous state of mind (see the description of the storm over the lake, stanzas 95–7).

Canto IV

The final Canto, although it states Byron's sufferings hardly less eloquently, reflects a serener mood. His stay in Venice had done much to restore his poise, his companion was the prosaic Hobhouse, not the volatile Shelley, and he had resumed his interest in history and antiquity. Much of the Canto is inspired by the civilisation of Italy and her men of genius in literature and art. It opens and closes with stately invocations to the realm of water, first to Venice, the bride of the Adriatic, and lastly to the Ocean, the element of which Byron felt himself the offspring. On his way south he pays especial homage to those Roman and Italian writers who upheld liberal ideals, or like himself suffered persecution and exile – Cicero, Livy, Dante, Petrarch, Tasso. In Rome itself his thoughts turn first to the imperial cycle, as Gibbon described it, of freedom, glory, wealth, corruption, barbarism. Secondly he reflects, echoing the Acropolis meditation of Canto II, on the theme of Time and its destruction of man-made empires, creeds and monuments. Thirdly he compares his own fate with that of the buildings around him, 'a ruin among ruins'.

Originally the structure of the Canto was comparatively simple, the first half up to stanza 77 covering the journey southward from Venice. The second half (stanzas 78–163) was devoted to Rome, with digressions on Byron's personal emotions and destiny, and the Canto concluded with the address to the Ocean. But the sixty stanzas which were later added and distributed throughout the Canto greatly complicated the design. As it now stands, two distinct approaches may be made. If we judge it in literary terms as the final section of a completed poem, it marks a transitional phase in Byron's development, a bridge between the desperate tensions of Canto III and *Manfred*, and the relaxed poise of *Beppo* (1818). Byron finally disposes of the mask of Harold and at the end of the *Pilgrimage* comes to see it as a means of expressing his view of the world. From this angle we see the piecemeal nature of the poem – a sequence of descriptions, reflections and declarations occasioned by landscapes, history, monuments and personal emotions – and the medley of styles and tones it contains, as reflections of the poet's viewpoint.

The other line of access is to read Canto IV as a record of Byron's state of mind and of his search for a guiding thread through the labyrinth of experience. This trail requires the reader to note the stanzas added to the original draft and their order of composition, since later additions often changed the final meaning of a passage. This approach helps the reader to follow the otherwise confusing oscillations of Byron's thought. It shows that despite repeated lapses into near despair, Byron ends, time and again, by reaffirming his belief in the redemptive force of art and of the creative imagination, in human freedom, in the search for truth and in the power of forgiveness. Thus the first affirmation is found in stanza 5, 'The beings of the mind are not of clay'; the second in stanza 98 which answers the disillusionment of 94; the third in stanza 127, which finds salvation in the power of independent thought to overcome the woes enumerated in the preceding verses – and this belief is pursued in the reflections inspired by St Peter's (stanzas 157–8); the fourth in stanzas 135 and 137 in which forgiveness turns the power of Nemesis to fruitful rather than destructive ends. Still, despite the thoughts occasioned by standing under St Peter's dome, the *Pilgrimage* does not bring Byron to religious faith. Delivered from the passions which have racked him, he is content with momentary insights and accepts what we now call an 'existential' view of life, whereby the individual sees himself as a free agent in a pre-determined and seemingly meaningless order of things, free to mingle with the universe and to be borne onward by the Ocean.

> We have had our reward and it is here,
> That we can yet feel gladden'd by the sun

(stanza 176)

The character of Childe Harold

Byron created the character of Harold (originally named Burun, the archaic form of Byron: Childe means young nobleman) because he needed a mouthpiece to present feelings and attitudes not necessarily acknowledged as his own. 'Anything is better than I, I, always I', he reminded his publisher. Harold is drawn as a caricature of the Romantic hero, a gloomy, self-absorbed young playboy, who has exhausted his pleasures and seeks escape in travel. At the start he is described in mock-archaic terms, as a young pilgrim en route for the Holy Land (I, stanzas 2–13): the verses which most clearly characterise Harold are those of the lyric 'To Inez', following stanza 84: here his fate is likened to that of the legendary Wandering Jew: 'And all my solace is to know/Whate'er betides, I've known the worst.' Contemporary commentators criticised Byron for attributing to Harold sentiments hardly distinguishable from his own, and modern critics have generally regarded him as a clumsy and ultimately pointless narrative device. Byron's public, uninterested in such technicalities, merely noted that Byron and Harold appeared to have much in common in their background and attributed Harold's libertine and misanthropic qualities to the poet. The two are most clearly differentiated in Canto I, when Harold is obviously undergoing misfortunes which Byron does not share. But by the end of Canto II, the satirical presentation of Harold has disappeared, and it is the poet's own griefs (as noted above) which are the centre of attention.

When Canto III appeared in 1816, Byron's contemporaries at once remarked upon the poet's identification of himself with Harold. Byron appeared to be living out the experience of his Romantic heroes: rejection by society was no longer an imagined suffering, but a real one. The beginning of the poem indicates how closely the two characters have come to resemble one another. Stanzas 2–8, written in the first person, refer to Byron: stanzas 8–16 nominally refer to Harold, but the two reports of experience are indistinguishable. Similarly, the sequence set in the Rhine valley (stanzas 50–5) and the Drachenfels lyric which follows, are nominally associated with Harold, but in fact relate to Byron's emotions concerning Augusta Leigh. In practice the distinction between

Byron and Harold is eliminated in this Canto and Byron formally recognises this in the Dedication to Canto IV. Further evidence is provided by the fact that the mockery of Romantic attitudes which enlivens Cantos I–II has disappeared in III and IV: Byron's stance at the emotional centre of the poem no longer permits of this detachment.

The *ottava rima* stanza

In September 1917 Byron read a new poem, *Whistlecraft* by J. H. Frere, written in *ottava rima*, the classical Italian stanza form, used in epic by Ariosto, but also by satirical poets such as Pulci, whom Byron had read. Byron also admired the verse of his friend John Merivale, who had experimented skilfully with the same stanza (both Frere and Merivale frequented John Murray's literary circle). The stanza, contains eight lines, usually ten-syllabled in English poetry, the first six rhymed alternately, the last a couplet: *ababbcc*. Frere's subject, a burlesque of King Arthur and his knights, was unimportant. What immediately attracted Byron was the ease and wit of the approach, the informal raconteur's technique, full of digressions and throw-away comments, the flexibility of the stanza with its run-on lines, the eccentric rhyming, and the clinching couplet, suitable either for a punch-line or a comic anti-climax.

By this date Byron had come to recognise that his *Tales* contained much over-pitched emotion and strained writing. It was time to stop pandering to the demand for this kind of product, and to dissociate himself from the image of the Byronic hero. So in *Beppo*, his first experiment in the new manner, he turns the formula for the *Turkish Tales* inside out. The hero, believed to be dead, has wandered abroad for years as a pirate, a slave, and a convert to Islam. But the poet ignores these 'Byronic' adventures. The plot turns on whether, after the return of the long-lost husband, his wife will resume their marriage, stay with her *amoroso*, or live alone. The flimsy story is merely a peg for the digressions, and Byron deliberately loses the narrative line to enlarge on the carnival, the Venetian character and attitude towards marriage, the attractions of Italian women, the climate and the language. This leads to comparisons with home, and a long catalogue of ironical compliments to the English way of life. The poem succeeds through its agile changes of subject: the effect is of a pianist improvising with dazzling skill and assurance. Byron was suddenly writing in a new voice, neither at the fever pitch of the *Tales*, nor in the sometimes stilted descriptive or reflective manner of *Harold*, but in his natural vocabulary and spontaneous conversational tone. He did not at once grasp the importance of the change, but in this light-hearted experiment he had laid the foundation for his mature comic and satirical poetry.

Don Juan

True to his general habits of working and his dislike of large-scale poetic or intellectual constructions, or 'systems', Byron gave little sign at the outset that in *Don Juan* he was embarking on the last and greatest creation of his career. He enquired how *Childe Harold*, Canto IV, and his verse story *Mazeppa* had been received, and merely said of his latest enterprise, 'It is intended to be a little quietly facetious about everything'. At the end of the Julia episode in Canto I, Byron digresses to discuss the nature of the whole work, 'My poem's epic, and is meant to be' (stanza 200), and lists the familiar hall-marks of the epic. It has twelve books, a gale at sea (*The Odyssey*), a list of ships (*The Iliad*), the theme is love and war (as in Homer, Virgil and the medieval and Renaissance epics). He is partly making fun of the conventional specifications and of the 'rules' of the Greek philosopher Aristotle (384–322BC). A year later he told Murray, who had asked for a plan, that he had no plan, only materials. Still his letters suggest that he had thought about what form a *modern* epic should take. If he was to attempt one, his gifts, clearly, were not for the heroic model, still less for the antiquarian kind, based on history or legend, such as Southey had written, but rather for the verse equivalent of the 'picaresque' type of novel (which does not conform to a regular plot, but merely follows the random travels and adventures of the hero), worldly in tone, colloquial in diction, loose in structure, assembled by accumulation as a coral reef rather than architecturally as a cathedral.

Byron often referred to *Don Juan* as a work which could be extended to any length. Shortly before his death he was joking about writing a hundred cantos and this view of the poem helps to explain his conception of the hero. He rejected the legendary image of Don Juan, the Satanic professional seducer, as he appears in Wolfgang Amadeus Mozart's (1756–91) opera. Instead he presents him as a young Everyman of modern times, a passive and malleable youth who mirrors the nature of the societies he encounters. In 1821, after finishing Canto V, Byron outlined his future plans. 'I meant to take him on a tour of Europe with a proper mixture of siege, battle and adventure. I meant to have made him a *cavaliere servente* in Italy, a cause for divorce in England, and a sentimental Werther-faced man in Germany, so as to show the different ridicules of the societies in each of these countries, and to have displayed him gradually *gâté* and *blasé* as he grew older, which is natural.'

Among the influences which shaped his original conception three are especially worth noting. The first was Henry Fielding's (1707–54) novel *Tom Jones* (1749), one of Byron's favourite novels, which its author had claimed to be a comic epic in prose set in a modern and naturalistic milieu. The second was Laurence Sterne's (1713–68) *Tristram Shandy* (1759–67), the novel which carried the device of digression to extraordinary lengths: Byron had already demonstrated his skill in digression in *Beppo*. The third was the Italian tradition of poetic improvisation before a live audience. Byron had listened to the famous *improvvisatore* Sgricci during his stay in Milan. Sgricci's verses were poetically quite undistinguished, but it was the poet's relation to his audience as sophisticated raconteur and entertainer which attracted Byron.

The sources for the poem were many and diverse. Canto I owes much to Byron's own early memories, imaginatively and mischievously adapted. The sketch of Donna Inez contains many characteristics of Byron's wife and a few of his mother's. Don José is a compound of both Byrons, father and son, and in Juan there are recollections of Byron's boyhood and upbringing. Julia's seduction of Juan and the scene of bedroom farce which ends the affair were based on stories Byron heard in Venice. For the shipwreck in Canto II Byron relied upon marine histories of the period, especially Dalzell's *Shipwrecks and Disasters at Sea*. The love affair with Haidée (Cantos II–IV) combines two traditions – first, the idyll of natural love uncorrupted by social conventions found in eighteenth-century romances such as Bernardin de Saint-Pierre's (1737–1814) *Paul et Virginie* (1787), and, second, Greek folk-tales which depict a girl punished by her family for falling in love with a stranger. The scenes in the harem (Cantos V–VI) are derived from French and Spanish stories and Near Eastern folklore describing the relationship of Oriental mistress and Christian slave. For the siege of Ismail (Cantos VII–VIII) Byron returns to the vividly realistic narrative of Canto II. He reports many of the details of the town's capture as they actually occurred and reproduces the history of the campaign contained in De Castelnau's *Essay on the History of Russia*. The same source supplied him with much of the background for the scenes at the court of Catherine the Great (Cantos IX–X). When the scene shifts to England Byron draws upon his recollections of London and country-house life as he had found them in the years 1811–16.

Nature of the poem

The most conspicuous and most original quality in *Don Juan* is the poem's perpetually shifting mood and tone, which change at a moment's notice from profundity to frivolity, tenderness to irony, horror to farce, an effect which Hazlitt described as 'the utter discontinuity of thoughts and feelings'. *Beppo* by comparison had been a mere trial balloon. *Don Juan* offers from the start a deliberate shock-treatment for the reader, often urbane, sometimes ruthless, but in any case quite new in English poetry, if we except the yoking of deliberately discordant images and emotions practised at times by Shakespeare and Donne. Byron, however, writes in this way not just for occasional effect, but as the keynote of the whole work. He does so because this mode of perception has come to colour his view of the world and of experience.

Various factors influence this approach. Byron is opposing the so-called Romantic trend in English poetry, which he saw as producing emotionally inflated, self-important verse, faults which he recognised in his own earlier writing. What he offers as an alternative is a sophisticated discourse between educated people. This assumes wit, absence of exaggeration, breadth of cultural and topical allusion, and unshockability, which demand a certain poise and detachment on the writer's part. Besides this he wished to see poetry upholding a truthful and objective view of life, and this involved an assault on 'the kingdom of cant', the rule of hypocrisy, self-deception, and false sentiment, alike in public and in private life. Seen in this context the poem's continual changes of tone do not result in superficiality or insincerity. *Don Juan* in fact expresses many of Byron's most passionately held convictions, for example his denunciation of war (Cantos VII–VIII), unless force of arms is used to restore human freedom. Rather the incessant changes of key should be seen as serving the pursuit of truth. If the poet's record of experience is to be genuine, he should not shrink from rendering discordant or incongruous elements. One of Byron's readers had objected to his juxtaposition of fun and gravity, on the grounds that we are never scorched and drenched at the same time. 'Blessings on his experience', Byron retorted, 'did he never spill a dish of tea in handing the cup to his charmer . . . to the great shame of his nankeen breeches? Did he never draw his foot out of a tub of too hot water damning his eyes and his valet's?'

Digressions

Byron succeeds in capturing the multiplicity of human experience through various devices, but chiefly through digression. He uses it not only for the normal purpose of varying the mood or speed of the narrative, but sometimes just for its own sake, partly as a display of virtuosity, partly to establish his new genre of 'conversational epic'. Thus in Canto I, before introducing the scene in Julia's bedroom, he starts with a reflection on the nature of first love and comparable experiences of pleasure: he then passes rapidly through vaccination, osteopathy, Congreve's rockets, galvanism and artificial respiration. Such monologues would quickly become tedious but for the lightness and mercurial quality of Byron's wit and his effortless mastery of the *ottava rima* stanza. His characters never lack eloquence (see for example Julia's scolding of her husband, stanzas 145–57) or her letter to Juan (stanzas 192–7), but he makes them speak with fairly predictable consistency, holding himself in reserve as commentator; this allows him to turn the mood upside down, or to sum up with some 'unpoetic', yet thoroughly topical allusion. Thus in sketching the character of the perfect wife (Donna Inez, stanza 17), his metaphors introduce a famous clock-maker and a hair oil of the period. He uses his prodigious command of rhyme to create double or triple rhymes, which with their feminine endings (unstressed final syllables) create the effect of a punch-line. See, for example, his address to Love (II, stanza 206):

> Thou mak'st the chaste connubial state precarious,
> And jestest with the brows of mightiest men:
> Caesar and Pompey, Mahomet, Belisarius,
> Have much employ'd the muse of History's pen:
> Their lives and fortunes were extremely various,
> Such worthies Time will never see again;
> Yet to these four in three things the same luck holds,
> They all were heroes, conquerors, and cuckolds.

This passage immediately follows the love scene between Juan and Haidée, the most consistently romantic passage in the whole poem.

Canto I

Canto I is in many ways a thoroughly representative section of *Don Juan*. It establishes Byron's unique blend of narrative, comment and digression, concentrates many of the salient features of the poem within a single episode, and sets the pattern of later events. We see Juan in his boyhood sheltered and manipulated by his mother, then in his adolescence seduced by a married woman. Thence in the later Cantos he passes from one situation of feminine dominance to another: even in the unreservedly romantic scenes with Haidée (Cantos II–IV) Juan is elevated by Haidée's status – he does not contribute to it. Canto I gives us the first taste of Byron's newly developed capacity to handle strongly felt personal experience with detachment, and to display his satirical insight into human illusions in terms of domestic comedy. Thus the plot exposes Inez's hypocrisy in throwing Juan and Julia together (stanza 101), and Julia's self-deception in playing with the idea of her husband's demise (stanza 84).

The Canto may also be read as a demonstration of Byron's skill in constructing a novel in verse. After a few remarks on the poet's choice of hero, the story is rapidly unfolded with only brief digressions up to stanza 117, when Juan and Julia become lovers. The poet as novelist requires less space than a prose fiction writer. Byron uses this freedom to employ what resembles a cinematic technique. He can telescope scenes of action, and devote his main attention to 'close-up' sequences, such as the character of Inez (stanzas 10–20, 23–39), the state of Julia's mind (stanzas 69–85), and of Juan's (86–97). After stanza 117, the narrative pauses, partly to provide the wide-ranging digression on pleasure, noted above. At stanza 136 the action resumes and the bedroom farce scene develops at ever increasing speed, reaching its climax at the end of the affair (stanza 188) when the key suddenly modulates to the pathos of Julia's letter. The remaining stanzas provide an epilogue, partly on the nature of the poem, but also to explain the poet's own frame of mind.

When Byron began to write *Don Juan* he had just passed thirty and his banishment from England was only two years behind him. These closing stanzas signal the lessons learned and the change of outlook which shapes the entire work, a shift from the involvement of Harold in Byron's adventures to the detachment of Byron-as-narrator from Juan's. In *Beppo* Byron had managed to create a hero who, if somewhat colourless, could not possibly be identified with the poet. In *Don Juan*, and in Canto I in particular, Byron's material is often autobiographical. His readers instantly connected Donna Inez with Lady Byron, and later the link between Juan's and Byron's own son-mother relationship also became apparent. The important difference in the poet's new stance is that Byron can now separate his boyish from his adult personality so that Juan is now distanced to a degree which was never possible with the heroes of the *Turkish Tales*. The hero of *Beppo* was almost pure invention, a difficult feat for Byron and probably unsustainable in a long poem. With Juan he can draw upon the rich resources of memory allowing his hero to re-enact experiences of his own. The price of this arrangement is that the development of Juan's character is very slight. He passes through many adventures, but his personality matures remarkably little. Byron as first-person narrator, on the other hand, acquires more and more authority, especially in the last cantos of the poem.

Reception of *Don Juan*

No other literary work of the period aroused anything approaching the scandal provoked by *Don Juan*. This in turn affected Byron and a short account of the reception of the poem will help us to appreciate its author's reaction. After Hobhouse and other close friends had read Canto I, Byron was advised that it would be impossible to publish or even to cut, since in Hobhouse's view the objectionable parts were in point of wit, humour and poetry the very best in the poem. His friends feared that Byron's absence had put him out of touch with public feeling and that publication would harm his standing irreparably. Byron argued that if *Don Juan* contained good poetry it would succeed, and that he would not give way to all the cant in Christendom. The first two

Cantos were published anonymously in July 1819. Hobhouse had not underestimated the reaction.

Don Juan was condemned on all sides, on moral rather than literary grounds. Byron's way of life, in politics, religion, family affairs and personal conduct, was seen as an outrage. In the first place, as a Whig he was regarded as a radical in home affairs, and soft on the national enemy, the French. In the second place, he consorted with atheists, such as Shelley: for the rest he had alienated his wife, chosen a life of depravity in Italy, and was suspected of homosexuality and incest. Not even Bertrand Russell or D. H. Lawrence in the present century earned such a triple crown of infamy. *Blackwood's Magazine* expressed the general view. It found beauty and genius in the poem, but also 'a more thorough infusion of genius and vice, power and profligacy than in any poem ever before written in England'. It was the author's evident poise and satisfaction which most offended. Byron was surprised by the violence of the reaction, but insisted that the poem was redeemed by its truth to nature. 'It may be profligate', he wrote, 'But is it not *life*, is it not the thing? Could any man have written it who had not lived in the world?'

Later in 1819 he wrote Cantos III–IV, which, perhaps under Teresa's influence, contained the most romantic scenes in the poem, but he admitted that his enthusiasm was cooling, and in 1820 he produced only Canto V. The next year Teresa, who had always disapproved of *Don Juan*, persuaded him to stop work on it. But with the publication of Cantos III–V he recovered his confidence. He kept his promise to Teresa, but by mid-1822 the picture had changed. Byron knew by then that *Don Juan* was being widely read, and he could now see it as a powerful weapon to combat the evils of war, oppression, hypocrisy, to which he was passionately opposed. In June 1822, shortly before Shelley's death, he resumed work, and for the next ten months threw all his energies into the poem, which from this point becomes predominantly critical of contemporary society – Cantos VII–VIII of war, Cantos IX–X of court life in Russia, and Cantos XI–XVI of England.

Conclusion

When the reader considers *Don Juan* as a whole, an obvious difference becomes apparent between the early and the later Cantos of the poem. In the first two episodes (Cantos I–IV) the personal relationships between Juan and Julia and Juan and Haidée eclipse all other interests. In the Turkish and Russian settings (Cantos V–VI and IX–X) a personal relationship exists, but is overshadowed by the autocratic roles of the Turkish Sultana and Russian Empress, and by the repressive societies to which they belong. Both in *The Corsair* and in *Don Juan* Byron reiterates the phrase 'Love is for the free'. Once in England, the plot slows almost to a standstill, digressions play an ever larger part and Byron's satire is mainly directed at social institutions (the marriage-market and the country-house visit). Finally the reader should remember the time-scheme of the poem, whereby Byron creates a sustained illusion, reminiscent of Marcel Proust's (1871–1922) novel cycle, *Remembrance of Things Past*: this illusion would have been more evident to Byron's contemporaries than to us. For the first five Cantos, since Byron's sources are literary rather than historical, the chronology is vague, almost mythical. But in Cantos VII–X, which find Juan at the siege of Ismail and the court of the Empress Catherine in her last years, the date must be about 1790. In Canto XII Juan watches the English Parliament in session, attended by George III and the then Prince of Wales, 'a finished gentleman from top to toe', who by 1823 had become the monstrously corpulent George IV. Byron is describing the life of a generation thirty years earlier, on the threshold of the French Revolution, a scene which gradually shades into his own lifetime, and this blending of perspectives deepens and enriches his picture.

The Vision of Judgment

The Vision of Judgment is artistically the most compact and sharply focused of all Byron's satires. It differs from the anecdotal approach of *Beppo* and the endlessly digressive manner of *Don Juan*: it follows a consistent theme and a clearly defined action in the mock-heroic convention. The poem is presented in the form of a dream-vision, but, as noted in the final stanza, a vision seen through a telescope, 'which kept my optics free from all delusion'. George III had reigned, nominally, for sixty years, nearly twice Byron's life-time. His death was a moment for historical stock-taking, and Byron was outraged by the obsequious flattery heaped upon his memory by Robert Southey (1774–1843). Byron's *Vision* is intended to set the record straight.

The king is treated with comparative charity throughout – 'A better farmer ne'er brushed dew from lawn'. He is a poor creature, but less to blame than those who defend him and the institution of monarchy. Byron's indignation and contempt are primarily directed at Southey, both as a man and as the embodiment of the ills to which Byron considered England especially vulnerable and which are summed up in the word *cant*, a profession of beliefs which society finds it convenient to maintain, though without any genuine conviction. First, cant political: Southey had begun life as a radical idealist, had tried to found a 'pantisocratic' commune in America, and had written a poem extolling the peasant revolutionary Wat Tyler. Thereafter he had turned against the French Revolution, become a creature of the Establishment, and was now trying to rewrite history by whitewashing the reign of George III. Secondly, cant religious: Southey invokes religious faith, but puts it to disreputable uses. He represents the mad old king as restored to health and making a triumphant entry into Heaven, hailed by such anti-monarchist immortals as Milton and Washington. He consigns George's political opponents to Hell: a genuine Christian would hope for their salvation. For all his own agnosticism, Byron evidently thought it positively blasphemous to depict God as blessing the record of George's reign. Thirdly, cant literary: Byron regarded Southey as the most contemptible member of the Lake school, who had degraded the art of poetry by accepting the office of Laureate, undertaking hack-work of all kinds, and embarking upon ill-judged experiments such as the clumsy unrhymed hexameters of *A Vision*. The main target of Alexander Pope's (1688–1744) great satire *The Dunciad* (1726) was another Laureate, Colley Cibber (1671–1757). Byron sees Southey as a classic example of the mediocre writer corrupted for short-term profit.

Having chosen the mock-epic style Byron sets the celestial scene in a framework which recognisably resembles that of *Paradise Lost*, but he presents angels, archangels and devils in a sophisticated and ironical light, showing the staff of Heaven as under-employed, while that of Hell is overworked thanks to the Napoleonic wars. For two-thirds of the poem (stanzas 16–84) Byron closely follows the sequence of events in Southey's *A Vision*, but he completely transforms their character. Thus while Southey hymns the glory of George's arrival in Heaven, Byron treats it as a non-event (stanzas 17–23). But he introduces Satan with true Miltonic grandeur, and presents his encounter with Michael with the majestic ceremonial appropriate to the meeting of great heads of state (stanzas 32–6). When the indictment against the king is developed (stanzas 42–9) – that 'he ever warred with freedom and the free', sought to maintain one tyranny in America and restore another in France, and caused immense bloodshed in the process – it becomes clear that Satan has been delegated to speak with the voice of Justice. As a life-long Whig, Byron was no respecter of the divine right of kings: it is thus a fine touch of irony that the Devil should have such a powerful case for the prosecution against God's anointed representative on earth.

With the arrival of the devil Asmodeus carrying Southey on his back, the tone of *The Vision* changes. The heavy artillery of satire is no longer needed: farce and belittling ridicule are substituted. Byron sees Southey as a highly placed hack to be put down because he presumes to sit in judgment, to decide who shall enter Heaven or Hell (stanza 101), and to scribble 'as if head-clerk to the Fates' (stanza 89). It is a consistent axiom in Byron's scheme of things that human good persists, while evil destroys itself – however long the process may take. Thus at the end Southey's deceitful attempts to rewrite history sink to the bottom, but

Southey himself, as corrupted matter, bobs up to the surface, before finally decomposing. George III is neither condemned nor acquitted. Byron could hardly bring in a verdict of guilty, and adroitly side-steps the issue by allowing him to slip into Heaven, unobserved because a nonentity.

In this poem Byron identifies himself most clearly not just as a rebel against monarchical authority, but as an aristocratic rebel. He shows a fellow-feeling for Satan to whom God has awarded a paltry triumph in granting him access to mankind – 'I think few worth damnation save their kings' (stanza 40). Byron champions freedom of speech, of worship (stanzas 48–9), of constitutional rule as against autocracy, of the writer's integrity against opportunism, but in each case he does this from the aristocratic standpoint.

The *Letters* and *Journals*

Byron is one of the most brilliant and many-sided letter-writers in the English language. 'I am not a cautious letter-writer', he declared, 'and generally say what comes uppermost at the moment.' Certainly his correspondence never suffers from timidity or pomposity. His letters and journals sometimes over-dramatise for the sake of effect, they are often self-critical or contradictory, but are always written with a disarming frankness and gusto. They are especially interesting for their revelation of how the melancholy and the exuberant elements in his nature could exist side by side, letters of high good humour coinciding with the composition of poems reflecting gloom or dejection. Usually it is Byron's high spirits which come through in his prose, but he notes that it is when people are most melancholy that they are most addicted to buffooning. Although he expresses his views on poetry clearly and forcefully, he seldom used his correspondence as a vehicle for lengthy discussion of poetry or the poet's function. His limitations as a critic are evident in the formal correspondence, resembling pamphlets rather than letters, in which he answered the attack on Pope made by the minor poet Bowles.

Byron excels in recording his impressions of foreign scenes and manners, and likewise of social encounters and human relationships: for the first see his superb description of the visit to Ali Pasha, written as early as 1809. His skill in describing society becomes especially prominent when, having settled in Venice, he begins to write for an audience in England, knowing that his accounts of the Venetian scene and of domestic comedies and scandals would be exchanged between his friends and read aloud in John Murray's office. Though he sometimes exaggerates, he knows well how to make his effects by understatement, as in his sketch of a noble but obstreperous family. 'The place is well and quiet and the children only scream in a low voice.' Besides creating an incomparably vivid impression of his life and times, the letters are indispensable to a closer understanding of Byron's poetry. They reveal the tempo at which Byron lived, they illuminate his use of language and the nature of his sensibility and of his inspiration, and how it differs from that of his contemporaries. A significant sentence on which to end is his remark, 'A man must travel and turmoil, or there is no existence'.

The plays

Byron wrote more plays than any of his English contemporaries and possessed a closer practical acquaintance with the theatre. He served on the Drury Lane Theatre committee during his London years and read many new plays in manuscript. Although he admired Shakespeare, he believed that the verse drama of his time should break away from the Elizabethan mould, and he tried to create a neo-classic drama. This was partly based on Aristotle's prescriptions for unity of place and time, and for an elevated subject-matter, mythological or historical. A more recent model was the Italian dramatist, Count Alfieri (1749–1803), to whose work and personality Byron was strongly drawn: Alfieri was a nobleman of liberal sympathies, he followed the neo-classical tradition, his plays were full of denunciations of tyranny and eulogies of freedom, he dealt with the subject of incest. Byron described his own plays as a theatre of the mind rather than of the stage.

His dramas fall into two broad categories: political tragedies based on historical subjects, of which the Venetian tragedies *Marino Falieri* and *The Two Foscari* are typical, and *Sardanapalus* the best constructed, and religious or philosophical plays of which *Manfred* and *Cain* are the most interesting. He could write fine set pieces of descriptive or rhetorical blank verse, or construct a lively ideological debate, as he does between Cain and Lucifer. But he lacked a sense of theatre, his handling of blank verse is often mechanical, and he found it difficult to compose plausible dialogue. He still deserves credit for employing a fresh approach to the problem of how to create a contemporary poetic drama, which should not be dominated by the Shakespearean model: his experiments take their place in the efforts towards this end which have been continued in the present century by W. B. Yeats and T. S. Eliot.

Part 4

Hints for study

IN MANY OF HIS WORKS Byron is writing a different species of poetry from that of his major Romantic contemporaries, Wordsworth and Coleridge, Shelley and Keats: there are more differences *in kind* between his poetry and theirs than there are resemblances. These arise partly from his pursuit of a very different pattern of life, but still more from a different conception of the nature of poetry and of the poet.

In a famous letter of 27 October 1818, Keats refers to the Poet as having no identity. He describes how, when he is in a room, the identity of his companions begins to press upon him, until he feels his own to be annihilated. Byron's stance is the very opposite of this position, and this factor calls for a different approach to his writing. Byron's individuality constantly obtrudes, even stands between reader and poem, so that a crucial part of the reader's response depends upon his exposure to this many-sided personality. This feeling is forced upon us through the constantly changing tone and content of his verse, even in such early work as Cantos I–II of *Childe Harold*.

The point may be illustrated by summarising the different attitudes which Byron takes up in various works, and even within the same work:

(i) The sensitive wanderer, chronicling his impressions of landscape or history: see *Childe Harold*, II, 86–8; III, 85–6; IV, 1–3.

(ii) The melodramatic exploiter of his emotions: see *The Giaour*; *The Corsair*; *Childe Harold*, III, 3–5.

(iii) The idealist, championing national liberation or attacking injustice: see *Childe Harold*, II, 74–6; IV, 98; *The Destruction of Sennacherib*; *The Isles of Greece*.

(iv) The patrician observer, moralising on history: see *Childe Harold*, III, 17–20; IV, 78–82.

(v) The satirist defending the literary values of the Augustan age: see *English Bards*.

(vi) The satirist subverting established social and political conventions: see *The Vision of Judgment*; *Don Juan*, Canto I.

(vii) The sophisticated raconteur and worldly-wise observer of human follies: see *Beppo*; *Don Juan*, Canto I.

The student will be able to add other roles to these.

The statement about Byron writing a different *kind* of poetry from his contemporaries applies especially to his late work, and above all to *Don Juan*. This poem makes it clear that *discordance* is a favourite Byronic effect. It is illustrated by the remark on the simultaneous experiences of 'scorching and drenching', but it is apparent even in the early Cantos of *Childe Harold*. Wordsworth had created a precedent by introducing material which the Augustans would have excluded as 'low' or 'mean'. Byron goes further, following Donne and Shakespeare, and anticipating the modern view that virtually *no* material can be excluded as unpoetic. 'After the lightning and the hurricane' says Hazlitt of *Don Juan*, 'we are introduced to the interior of the cabin and the contents of the wash-hand basins.' Discordance, in this sense of juxtaposing incongruous elements, is an effect deliberately practised in the late poems. But there is another kind, which springs from a temperamental trait, and again marks off Byron from his Romantic contemporaries, a mocking concealment or denial of his real emotions for fear of exposing them to scorn or ridicule. It is exemplified in the epigram he wrote shortly before his last journey to Greece.

> When a man hath no freedom to fight for at home
> Let him combat for that of his neighbours
> Let him think of the glories of Greece and of Rome,
> And get knocked on the head for his labours.

You will find examples of this attitude of mind throughout Byron's work.

To understand Byron's verse well requires more than an exclusively verbal study of the text. Because he is a less self-effacing artist than Keats, we need, as it were, a bi-focal view, looking at the man for the sake of the work and vice versa. You should possess at least an outline of Byron's movements and attachments in London, Greece and Italy, since these changing circumstances had an unmistakable influence on what he wrote and when he wrote it. It is also very desirable to gain some knowledge of the *Letters* and *Journals*. Apart from their literary merit, which is great, their descriptive prose passages throw a light on the character of his poetry, and his highly idiosyncratic way of reporting experience.

Because of Byron's preoccupation with the practical and worldly aspects of living, and because of his gifts for satire and for social comedy, his poems are often packed with contemporary and historical allusions, *The Vision of Judgment* and *Don Juan* quite exceptionally so. This makes a reference book such as *The Oxford Companion to English Literature* and a good dictionary very helpful aids to understanding, especially since Byron is fond of investing an apparently simple word with a pun or a *double-entendre*.

Preparing for an examination

The study of a major poet is necessarily a gradual process, to be continued as long as is practicable. The knowledge you obtain is cumulative: as your familiarity grows, you come to recognise – even in unlikely places – resemblances and significant qualities shared between works, major and minor. It is to test this familiarity – the ability to grasp selected passages, to interpret poems as a whole, and to recognise the author's distinctive characteristics – that you are being examined. These principles of course apply to the study of poetry generally: they certainly do to Byron's, where steady and systematic preparation is indispensable. One reason for this is that Byron was not a creator of small, compact masterpieces. He lacked the ability, even in his best work, to concentrate his effects, and needs to be read at length.

Byron's work might appear impossibly daunting for its sheer bulk and variety. However to familiarise yourself with a representative cross-section should be well within your grasp. Better still if you can extend your range, but you must have a close knowledge of the essential poems on your list rather than a distant acquaintance with a large number. Those you should know well include:

LYRICS: at least those in the Skelton edition, as well as *Hebrew Melodies*, which are best read as a song cycle;

NARRATIVES: two of those written before 1816 and two after, as well as *Beppo* as the first of the *ottava rima* poems;

SATIRES: *The Vision of Judgment* and passages from poems written in couplets, for example, *English Bards* and *The Waltz*; also selections from *Childe Harold* and from *Don Juan*.

The advice which follows is offered with examination conditions in mind. For a class-room essay you have access to books for purposes of reference and quotation, but when preparing for an examination there are obvious difficulties in memorising the work of a poet who writes at such length. You can memorise a few of the well-known short lyrics, and those passages in *Childe Harold* which are especially revealing of Byron's thought on poetry and life, for example, III, 6, 'Tis to create ...'; IV, 5, 'The beings of the mind ...'; IV, 137, 'But I have lived ...'; also perhaps a few stanzas from *Don Juan* – some are noted below – which show significant contrasts in style.

Lyrics:

Byron wrote of his schooldays, 'My qualities were much more oratorical than poetical.' You might use this as a trial question to judge his performance as a lyrical poet. In general the virtues of his lyrics are directness, clarity, resonance: he is not a poet of atmosphere, of fleeting or subtle impressions. The beat is often so regular as to be near-mechanical, the thought so direct that it could without difficulty be expressed in prose. Analyse one of the rare exceptions, 'There be none of beauty's daughters', to discover how Byron is capable of remarkable melodic beauty and metrical subtlety, and how seldom he attempts these. On the credit side, consider his skill in telling a story in lyric form, for example, 'The Vision of Belshazzar' (*Hebrew Melodies*), or charging a lyric with drama, as in the lyrical interludes in *Childe Harold*. Consider the above in relation to specimen question 10, below.

Narratives:
The *Turkish Tales* and later narratives were among the first of Byron's poems to be translated, and his fame in non-English-speaking countries still rests to a surprising extent upon them. This is partly because of their relatively simple language and the absence of complex allusions, compared to the *ottava rima* poems. Consider the resemblances and differences between Childe Harold and the heroes of the *Tales*; also what drew Byron to the subjects of the *Tales*, and what would have been their attraction to his contemporaries. The narratives will not be adequately understood if you read no more than the short extracts in the Skelton edition. Without needing to study the whole text intensively, you must read these poems through to master the outline of the plot, fit the extract into its context, and see the story as a whole. The poems survive mainly because of Byron's irresistible energy in narration and vigour of expression. Remember that a poem, however uneven in workmanship, is always a metrical composition. Byron experimented widely with rhymed couplets, the four-foot line, the anapaestic ($\cup \cup -$) line, and in *The Bride of Abydos* with all three. Analyse what effects of emotional tone, or variations in the pace of the story he is trying to achieve. Thus, in *The Bride of Abydos* the anapaestic line creates a highly languorous effect, in *The Destruction of Sennacherib* the opposite.

Childe Harold:
This is a difficult poem to see as a whole, especially Cantos III–IV. Although there is nominally a movement from place to place, Byron's thought sometimes meanders confusingly, or doubles back on itself. To construct an outline which you can hold in your memory, you may find it helpful to break up each Canto into separate sections, centred upon places or historical events, or separate sequences of thought. Some guidelines to this approach are offered in Part 3.

Specimen answers

(1) Compare and contrast the handling of the narrative and the choice of language and metre in *The Corsair* and *The Prisoner of Chillon*.

You could begin by mentioning the very different origins and themes of the two poems. The first was written in 1813, when Byron's inspiration was still dominated by his memories of the Near East, and it has much in common with the other *Turkish Tales*. The second dates from June 1816, when Byron was beginning to put the melodramatic type of tale behind him. Through his friendship with Shelley, he had become sympathetic to the Wordsworthian low-keyed mode of narration. In *The Prisoner* he sets out to write a comparatively uneventful, yet realistic tale on the destructive effects of long imprisonment. There is an organic difference between the two poems, which is reflected in the choice of language and imagery. At the opening of Canto I of *The Corsair*, Byron at once establishes the outdoor masculine world of his hero. These lines exult in Conrad's freedom to roam the seas and in the reckless courage on which it depends. The rhymed couplets set a headlong pace, which accords with the impetuous decision to sail on a raid that night. Against this world is set the enclosed feminine world of Medora, Conrad's neglected mistress. In the same Canto the couplet is used to create a completely different tune and tempo in Medora's song, 'Deep in my soul that tender secret dwells'. At the beginning of Canto III the masculine and feminine elements are contrasted in the description of the setting of the sun and the rising of the moon over Athens. Towards the end of Canto III, when Conrad returns, as he hopes, to Medora, Byron again quickens the pace, using such devices as accumulated verbs and alliteration

> He waits not, looks not, leaps into the wave
> Strives through the surge, bestrides the beach . . .

Then at the climax of the poem, the discovery of Medora, dead, the couplet is transformed to create a sombre, elegiac rhythm, broken by heavy pauses in mid-line:

> He ask'd no question, all was answered now . . .
> It was enough she died: what reck'd it how?

In *The Prisoner* the general effect is almost diametrically opposite. Instead of the violent energy of *The Corsair*, we have a completely static situation, the hero's courage being demonstrated in endurance, not in action. The theme, which is centred upon the loss of liberty and its effect on the human spirit, is unfolded without illusions or histrionics.

Metrically speaking, the couplets of *The Corsair* lend themselves to formal characterisation in the Augustan manner – 'Betray'd too early and beguil'd too long'. The four-foot measure of *The Prisoner* is associated with ballads and with deliberately simplified tales such as Wordsworth's *The Thorn*. Byron has correspondingly simplified his vocabulary, and moved closer to what Wordsworth terms 'a selection of the language really used by men'. He is not at once at home in this style: some lines clearly contain padding

I saw it silently decline –
And so perchance in sooth did mine

and he falls at times into a Wordsworthian repetition of simple, even trite, epithets and images

But in it there were three tall trees,
And o'er it blew the morning breeze
And by it there were waters flowing
And on it there were young flowers growing

– what else could flow by an islet but water?

Compared with the effects Coleridge could create with this metre, Byron's choice of noun and epithet often sounds flat. But he achieves an altogether deeper insight than before into his hero's state of mind, and he sounds a note of realism which is quite new in his poetry when he pictures Bonnivard's limbs as 'rusted with a vile repose', and describes the slow torture of solitary confinement as 'vacancy absorbing space/And fixedness without a place'. By the final section of the poem his mastery of his medium is becoming evident. He produces one of its most arresting images, the prisoner watching the spiders 'at their sullen trade', and the anti-climax of Bonnivard's sudden and arbitrary release is most skilfully prepared.

---

(2) How would you defend *The Vision of Judgment* against the charge that it is a mere lampoon or malicious personal attack on Southey?

Many of the masterpieces of the greatest satirists – Juvenal, Dryden, Pope – were occasioned by personal animosity against some individual, who was seen as embodying the vices of the age. But if the attack is no more than personal, its interest quickly fades. Only satire aimed at subjects of lasting concern will continue to find readers. The Dedication to *Don Juan is* an explicit personal attack on Southey. It scores a number of brilliant hits, but it is far less widely known than *The Vision*, and nobody's appreciation of *Don Juan* will suffer much for not having read it.

Byron and Southey were undeniably enemies of long standing. During Byron's exile, Southey had attacked his character both in speech and in writing, and now he published what Byron considered a ludicrously bad poem. However, much of Byron's *Vision* is aimed less at Southey in person than at what he was a part of. In Byron's eyes Southey was a defender of the Tory Establishment, which stood for excessive privilege, repression of civil rights, religious intolerance, adulation of the monarchy, resistance to change at home and abroad. These were Byron's political and social targets. On the literary front he disliked the Lake School in general and Southey as its most mediocre representative.

He despised him further for having bartered his youthful liberal principles for patronage, and, having obtained the Laureateship, degrading it by making it a vehicle for governmental propaganda.

He lists Southey's successive betrayals in stanza 97:

He had written praises of a regicide;
  He had written praises of all kings whatever;
He had written for republics far and wide,
  And then against them bitterer than ever;
For pantisocracy he once had cried
  Aloud, a scheme less moral than 'twas clever;
Then grew a hearty anti-jacobin –
Had turn'd his coat – and would have turn'd his skin.

Byron's main theme in *The Vision* is historical – Judgment Day after the sixty-year reign of George III – and it was Southey's attempt to rewrite history which brought him into the poem. After so many years of Tory rule, judgment must have seemed an almost sacred task to a life-long Whig such as Byron. But although his poem is intended to arouse derision against the monarchy, he writes with control and discrimination. He does not spare the system, but he treats the person of the king with some compassion.

His most original achievement in this satire is his presentation of Satan. He is characterised not as the Devil malevolently claiming a king's soul for damnation, but as a Public Prosecutor striving to uphold principles which Divine Justice might be expected to approve. His indictment accuses the king of having oppressed free men, encouraged religious intolerance and waged unjust wars. This part of the satire is developed on a high moral and philosophical plane. Satan is related to Prometheus and other types of Byronic hero, cast out because they will not submit to the authority of a Supreme Being. *The Vision of Judgment*, then, is designed on a far larger scale than a mere personal attack.

Specimen questions

(1) 'The last of the Augustans'. Consider the adequacy of this description of Byron.

(2) What appealed in Byron to his contemporaries and what appeals to us today?

(3) Is it necessary to know Byron's life-story to interpret his poetry? Is it accurate or sufficient commentary to call Byron's best poetry satire?

(4) Keats wrote disapprovingly of Byron's poetry, 'He describes what he sees: I describe what I imagine. Mine is the hardest task.' Is this a fair judgment of Byron?

(5) Wordsworth, Shelley and Keats all responded with indignation against the injustices of their time. So too did Byron, but he is alone among the major Romantics in using laughter as a weapon of protest. Discuss with reference to Byron's satires and comic narratives.

(6) 'As long as I wrote the exaggerated nonsense which has corrupted the public taste, they applauded me to the echo.' Is this a fair estimate of the poetry Byron wrote before *Don Juan*?

(7) 'Scott and Byron were traditionally regarded as Romantic writers, but we have come to see their main achievements as anti-Romantic.' Discuss with reference to Byron.

(8) By what tokens do you recognise the author of *Childe Harold* in *Don Juan*?

(9) 'Intensity is the great and prominent distinction of Lord Byron's writings. He seldom gets beyond force of style, nor has he produced any regular work or masterly whole. He does not prepare a plan beforehand, nor revise and retouch what he has written with polished accuracy. His only object seems to be to stimulate himself and his readers for the moment.' (Hazlitt) Would you defend Byron against these criticisms?

(10) 'The delicacy of Byron's romantic lyrics is evidence that he is far from being a careless artist.' Discuss.

(11) 'Byron's satire is justified by a deep seriousness; it is not just to giggle and make giggle.' Discuss with reference to *The Vision of Judgment* and *Don Juan*.

(12) 'Byron's genius is predominantly a destructive genius.' How far would you agree with this judgment?

Part 5

Suggestions for further reading

The texts

The Works of Lord Byron: Poetry, 6 vols, edited by E. H. Coleridge, John Murray, London, 1898–1904. This edition is extensively annotated and is invaluable for explaining the numerous topical allusions in Byron's poetry. Pending the completion of the Clarendon Press edition, it is indispensable for the understanding of the later poems.

Lord Byron: The Complete Poetical Works, edited by Jerome J. McGann, Clarendon Press, Oxford, 1980– . The editor has added eighty-six poems or poetic fragments, many of them previously unpublished, removed five as spurious, and tackled the problem of the numerous corrupt readings contained in all earlier editions. This edition is well annotated and includes Byron's own notes.

Selected Poems of Byron, edited by Robin Skelton, Poetry Bookshelf series, Heinemann Educational Books, London, 1964, repr. 1980. It contains complete texts of *The Siege of Corinth*, *The Prisoner of Chillon*, *The Vision of Judgment* and *Don Juan*, Canto I, with extracts from *Childe Harold*, Canto IV, and other narrative poems and complete texts of many lyrics.

Byron: Poetical Works, Oxford Standard Authors edition. Edited by F. Page, Oxford University Press, London, 1904: new edition corrected by John Jump, 1970. A general one-volume edition of the *Poetical Works*, including the plays. This is needed for reading beyond the extracts printed in the Skelton edition; annotation is limited to Byron's own notes.

The Works of Lord Byron: Letters and Journals, 5 vols, edited by R. E. Protheroe, John Murray, London, 1901. This edition has been superseded by Professor Marchand's, but contains valuable notes and also includes in Vol. 5 the important controversy between Byron and the Rev. W. L. Bowles on the poetry of Pope.

Byron: Letters and Journals, 12 vols, edited by Professor L. A. Marchand, John Murray, London, 1973–82. The standard edition, which contains many previously unpublished letters and has eliminated many spurious ones. Well annotated.

Byron: A Self Portrait, 2 vols, edited by Peter Quennell, John Murray, London, 1950. A well-chosen selection of the *Letters* and *Journals*.

Lord Byron: Selected Letters and Journals, edited by Professor L. A. Marchand, John Murray, London, 1982. A compendious one-volume selection from the standard edition

Secondary works

BLESSINGTON, COUNTESS OF: *Conversations with Lord Byron*, London, 1834.
TRELAWNY, E. J.: *Recollections of the Last Days of Byron, Shelley and the Author*, London, 1858. Vivid but sometimes unreliable memoirs of the two poets in Italy and Greece.
TRELAWNY, E. J.: *Records of Shelley, Byron and the Author*, London, 1878. An expanded edition of the *Recollections of the Last Days.*

Biography

CLINE, C. L.: *Byron, Shelley and Their Pisan Circle*, John Murray, London, 1952. A study of the year 1821–2.
MARCHAND, L. A.: *Byron: A Biography*, 3 vols, John Murray, London, 1957. The fullest and most scholarly study. Abridged to one volume as *Byron: A Portrait*, 1971.
MOORE, D. L.: *The Late Lord Byron*, John Murray, London, 1961. A thorough investigation of Byron's reputation after his death.
NICOLSON, H.: *Byron: The Last Journey*, Constable, London, 1924. An account of Byron's final visit to Greece.
QUENNEL, P.: *Byron: The Years of Fame. Byron in Italy*, one-volume edition, Collins, London, 1974. A brilliant portrait of Byron's character and environment during the years 1811–23.

Criticism

ARNOLD, M.: *Essays in Criticism*, Second Series, London, 1888.
BLACKSTONE, B.: *Byron: A Survey*, Longman, London, 1975. Critical appreciations of the whole range of Byron's verse.
ELIOT, T. S.: *On Poetry and Poets*, Faber, London, 1957.
JOSEPH, M. K.: *Byron the Poet*, Gollancz, London, 1964. An important critical study of the character and technique of Byron's verse, excluding the lyrics.
LEAVIS, F. R.: *Revaluation*, Chatto and Windus, London, 1936. Contains an important essay on Byron's satire.
MACAULAY, T. B.: *Critical and Historical Essays*, London, 1842.
McGANN, J. J.: *Fiery Dust: Byron's Poetic Development*, University of Chicago Press, Chicago, 1968. Interpretative essays on Byron's early verse, *Childe Harold*, four of the Tales, five plays and *Don Juan*.

MARCHAND, L. A.: *Byron's Poetry: A Critical Introduction*, John Murray, London, 1965. Critical appreciations of Byron's lyrics, narratives and satires.

RUTHERFORD, A.: *Byron: A Critical Study*, Oliver and Boyd, Edinburgh, 1961. An excellent critical survey of Byron's narrative, satirical and dramatic verse.

RUTHERFORD, A. (ED.): *Byron: The Critical Heritage*, Routledge, London, 1970. A critical anthology which documents the reception of Byron's poetry from 1808 to 1909.

The author of these notes

IAN SCOTT-KILVERT studied Classics at Harrow School and graduated in English Literature at the University of Cambridge. He was director of the Literature Department of the British Council (1962–77) and is general editor of the *Writers and their Work* series, to which he contributed essays on *John Webster* and *A. E. Housman*. He is the translator of *The Rise and Fall of Athens*, *Makers of Rome*, and *The Age of Alexander* (successive volumes of Plutarch's *Lives*), *The Rise of the Roman Empire* (the *Histories* of Polybius), *The Reign of Augustus* (Cassius Dio) and *The Civil Wars* (Appian), all in the Penguin Classics series. He is co-chairman of the Byron Society.

York Notes: list of titles

CHINUA ACHEBE
Things Fall Apart

EDWARD ALBEE
Who's Afraid of Virginia Woolf?

MARGARET ATWOOD
Cat's Eye
The Handmaid's Tale

W. H. AUDEN
Selected Poems

JANE AUSTEN
Emma
Mansfield Park
Northanger Abbey
Persuasion
Pride and Prejudice
Sense and Sensibility

SAMUEL BECKETT
Waiting for Godot

ALAN BENNETT
Talking Heads

ARNOLD BENNETT
The Card

JOHN BETJEMAN
Selected Poems

WILLIAM BLAKE
Songs of Innocence, Songs of Experience

ROBERT BOLT
A Man For All Seasons

CHARLOTTE BRONTË
Jane Eyre

EMILY BRONTË
Wuthering Heights

ROBERT BURNS
Selected Poems

BYRON
Selected Poems

GEOFFREY CHAUCER
The Franklin's Tale
The Knight's Tale
The Merchant's Tale
The Miller's Tale
The Nun's Priest's Tale
The Pardoner's Tale
Prologue to the Canterbury Tales
The Wife of Bath's Tale

SAMUEL TAYLOR COLERIDGE
Selected Poems

JOSEPH CONRAD
Heart of Darkness

DANIEL DEFOE
Moll Flanders
Robinson Crusoe

SHELAGH DELANEY
A Taste of Honey

CHARLES DICKENS
Bleak House
David Copperfield
Great Expectations
Hard Times
Oliver Twist

EMILY DICKINSON
Selected Poems

JOHN DONNE
Selected Poems

DOUGLAS DUNN
Selected Poems

GEORGE ELIOT
Middlemarch
The Mill on the Floss
Silas Marner

T. S. ELIOT
Four Quartets
Selected Poems
The Waste Land

HENRY FIELDING
Joseph Andrews

F. SCOTT FITZGERALD
The Great Gatsby

GUSTAVE FLAUBERT
Madame Bovary

E. M. FORSTER
Howards End
A Passage to India

JOHN FOWLES
The French Lieutenant's Woman

BRIAN FRIEL
Translations

ELIZABETH GASKELL
North and South

WILLIAM GOLDING
Lord of the Flies

OLIVER GOLDSMITH
She Stoops to Conquer

GRAHAM GREENE
Brighton Rock
The Heart of the Matter
The Power and the Glory

THOMAS HARDY
Far from the Madding Crowd
Jude the Obscure
The Mayor of Casterbridge
The Return of the Native
Selected Poems
Tess of the D'Urbervilles

L. P. HARTLEY
The Go-Between

NATHANIEL HAWTHORNE
The Scarlet Letter

SEAMUS HEANEY
Selected Poems

ERNEST HEMINGWAY
A Farewell to Arms
The Old Man and the Sea

SUSAN HILL
I'm the King of the Castle

HOMER
The Iliad
The Odyssey

GERARD MANLEY HOPKINS
Selected Poems

TED HUGHES
Selected Poems

ALDOUS HUXLEY
Brave New World

HENRY JAMES
The Portrait of a Lady

BEN JONSON
The Alchemist
Volpone

JAMES JOYCE
Dubliners
A Portrait of the Artist as a Young Man

JOHN KEATS
Selected Poems

PHILIP LARKIN
Selected Poems

D. H. LAWRENCE
The Rainbow
Selected Short Stories
Sons and Lovers
Women in Love

HARPER LEE
To Kill a Mockingbird

LAURIE LEE
Cider with Rosie

CHRISTOPHER MARLOWE
Doctor Faustus

ARTHUR MILLER
The Crucible
Death of a Salesman
A View from the Bridge

JOHN MILTON
Paradise Lost I & II
Paradise Lost IV & IX

TONI MORRISON
Beloved

SEAN O'CASEY
Juno and the Paycock

GEORGE ORWELL
Animal Farm
Nineteen Eighty-four

JOHN OSBORNE
Look Back in Anger

WILFRED OWEN
Selected Poems

HAROLD PINTER
The Caretaker

SYLVIA PLATH
Selected Works

POETRY OF THE FIRST WORLD WAR

ALEXANDER POPE
Selected Poems

J. B. PRIESTLEY
An Inspector Calls

JEAN RHYS
The Wide Sargasso Sea

J. D. SALINGER
The Catcher in the Rye

WILLIAM SHAKESPEARE
Antony and Cleopatra
As You Like It
Coriolanus
Hamlet
Henry IV Part I
Henry IV Part II
Henry V
Julius Caesar
King Lear
Macbeth
Measure for Measure
The Merchant of Venice
A Midsummer Night's Dream
Much Ado About Nothing
Othello
Richard II
Richard III
Romeo and Juliet
Sonnets
The Taming of the Shrew
The Tempest
Twelfth Night
The Winter's Tale

GEORGE BERNARD SHAW
Arms and the Man
Pygmalion
Saint Joan

MARY SHELLEY
Frankenstein

RICHARD BRINSLEY SHERIDAN
The Rivals

R. C. SHERRIFF
Journey's End

MURIEL SPARK
The Prime of Miss Jean Brodie

JOHN STEINBECK
The Grapes of Wrath
Of Mice and Men
The Pearl

TOM STOPPARD
Rosencrantz and Guildenstern are Dead

JONATHAN SWIFT
Gulliver's Travels

JOHN MILLINGTON SYNGE
The Playboy of the Western World

MILDRED D. TAYLOR
Roll of Thunder, Hear My Cry

W. M. THACKERAY
Vanity Fair

MARK TWAIN
Huckleberry Finn

VIRGIL
The Aeneid

DEREK WALCOTT
Selected Poems

ALICE WALKER
The Color Purple

JOHN WEBSTER
The Duchess of Malfi

OSCAR WILDE
The Importance of Being Earnest

TENNESSEE WILLIAMS
Cat on a Hot Tin Roof
A Streetcar Named Desire

VIRGINIA WOOLF
Mrs Dalloway
To the Lighthouse

WILLIAM WORDSWORTH
Selected Poems

W. B. YEATS
Selected Poems